Adventure Motorcycle
Maintenance
Manual

Published in October 2012

A catalogue record for this book is available from the British Library

ISBN 978 0 85733 059 8

Library of Congress catalog card no 2011930600

Published by Haynes Publishing,
Sparkford, Yeovil, Somerset BA22 7JJ, UK
Tel: +44 1963 442030 Fax: +44 1963 440001
E-mail: sales@haynes.co.uk
Website: www.haynes.co.uk

Haynes North America Inc.,
861 Lawrence Drive, Newbury Park,
California 91320, USA

Printed in the USA by Odcombe Press LP,
1299 Bridgestone Parkway, La Vergne, TN 37086

📷 Touratech

Dedication

For my wife Sue, whose love, support, encouragement and perfect timing with the tea and biscuits kept me going through so many dark nights at the keyboard.

Acknowledgements

The author would like to thank the following people for their support and expertise:

- **Steve Mills**
- **Tim Cheetham**
- **Steve Spring**
- **Pat King**
- **Jordan Thomas**

Ian Newham – Yuasa Battery UK
Mike Chadwick – Custom Cruisers
Jon Parkes – Rugged Roads
Norman Birtles – Nippy Normans Ltd
Tony Starling – StarCom (Tecstar Electronics Ltd)
Skidmarx, Weymouth
Ross Walker – KTM UK Ltd
Nick Muddle – Scottoiler Ltd
Wally and the team at CW Motorcycles, Dorchester

All images on pages 44–103 and 124–151 supplied by the author or Haynes unless otherwise credited

The author would also like to extend special thanks to:

Lee Parsons (Senior Designer) and **Steve Rendle** (Commissioning Editor) at Haynes Publishing for their insight, guidance and vision in bringing the whole project together.
Robert Wicks (Adventure Motorcyclist and Thoroughly Good Egg) for planting the seed of the idea and being a great friend.
Mark Hughes Editorial Director at Haynes Publishing for his continual support and forbearance during this project.

Adventure Motorcycle
Maintenance
Manual

The essential manual to the skills
needed to maintain and prepare a
modern adventure motorcycle

Greg Baker
Foreword by **Robert Wicks**

Service procedures ▪ **Tour preparation** ▪ **Fitting accessories** ▪ **Roadside maintenance and repairs**

Contents

Foreword by Robert Wicks

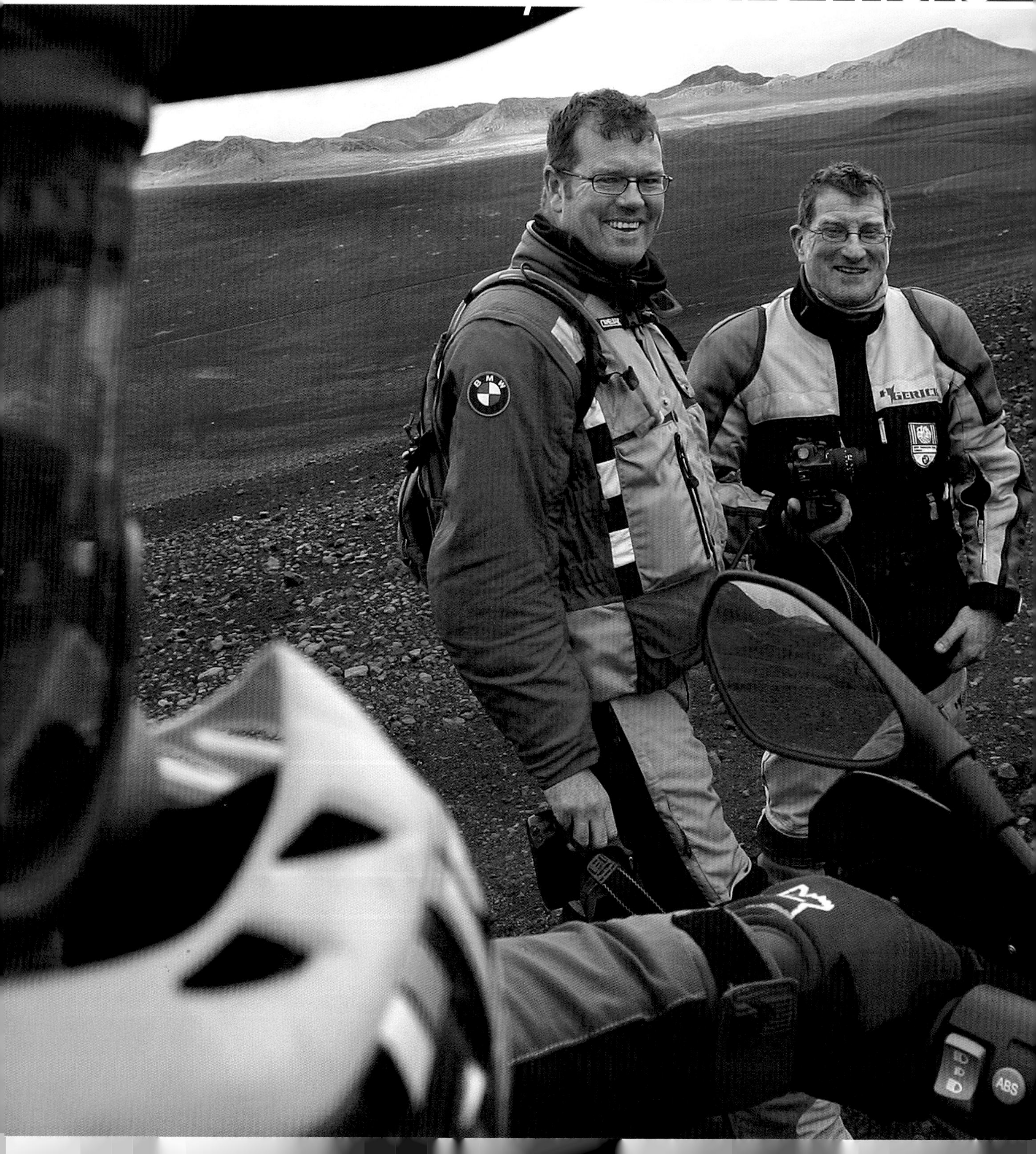

By his own admission, acclaimed author Robert Pirsig said his 1974 philosophical novel, *Zen and the Art of Motorcycle Maintenance*, 'should in no way be associated with that great body of factual information relating to orthodox Zen Buddhist practice. It's not very factual on motorcycles, either.' Well, there's no reference to Zen Buddhist practices in this book either, but Greg has certainly created a wealth of invaluable information on the subject matter of adventure motorcycle maintenance.

Embarking on an adventure ride is a substantial undertaking and just getting everything prepared is one thing. Preparing yourself for life on the road and being in the best position possible to make even the most elementary of running repairs to help keep you moving is something completely different.

By our very nature, it is fair to say that adventure motorcyclists are more likely to have a reasonable understanding of maintenance techniques simply because we need to be as self-sufficient as possible out on the road. That said, there are newcomers to this wonderful pastime who need information and a fair few of the 'regulars' who could do with some specialist insight. Not everyone has a broad technical skill-set and motorcycles today are more and more complex, with advanced electronics now the norm, particularly on the larger machines.

Maintaining your bike while travelling is one of the keys to a successful adventure. I always encourage intrepid adventurers to know as much about their motorcycle as possible. You can do this by reading the bike's manual, enrolling on a maintenance course, doing web research, or simply getting help and advice from a local garage or friend. But before you do any of that, take the time to read this book from cover to cover, and then read it again.

With this latest book, the fifth in the acclaimed Haynes Adventure Motorcycling series, Greg brings a new level of understanding to subject matter that is often neglected, misunderstood or disregarded because it is simply 'too technical'. *Adventure Motorcycle Maintenance Manual* is based on years of experience and countless adventures, and is written with a clarity and sense of purpose that make the subject matter interesting, engaging and tangible.

← **Most people would be fazed by a mechanical problem right at the beginning of a trip – Greg calmly and methodically working his way through the electrics of his KTM.**
Robert Wicks

← **Robert Wicks and Greg Baker during photography for their book *Adventure Riding Techniques*.**
Thorvaldur Orn Kristmundsson

I recall the night before Greg and I embarked on an adventure in the Sahara. He was working into the early hours of the morning in the dim light of a Moroccan garage to get to the bottom of a complicated electrical fault on his KTM 950 that could have jeopardised our entire adventure. Needless to say he found the problem and we took to the road a few hours later.

This book adopts a practical approach to the subject matter and covers setting up a workshop, all key areas of essential maintenance, pre-trip preparation, advice on tools and spares, fitting specialist parts and, most importantly, dealing with technical issues on the road.

Out on the trail, if your motorcycle will not move, neither will you, so get reading – it may just be that wisdom from these pages will get you back on track.

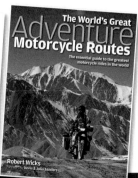

Overlanding

Noun; definition: self-reliant overland travel to remote destinations where the journey is the principal goal.

We are in a changing world. It changes around us, and it can change us. We are fortunate to live in a time when we have the opportunity to be truly global with our aspirations, and never before has the world been so accessible. This accessibility can be bought for a price, with many choosing to fly or sail to a tourist 'resort' of their choice. But, for a few of us, this option would be quite literally the last resort, as we have chosen an adventure motorcycle as our means of transport.

Adventure motorcycling is not entirely a new phenomenon, however, and history reveals pioneers of overlanding from the very early days of motorised transport. In 1932, at the age of 23, Robert Fulton Jnr embarked on a trip which over the following 18 months took him from London to Tokyo, riding his 600cc Douglas twin-cylinder motorcycle through Europe to Turkey, then Syria, Iraq, Afghanistan, India, Sumatra, Malaysia, Siam, Indonesia and China, before finally ending his adventure in Japan.

Perhaps more remarkable is the tale of two English women, Theresa Wallach and Florence Blenkiron, who in 1935 piloted their 600cc Model 100 Panther sidecar and trailer combination from London to Cape Town. With nothing short of iron determination and a clear objective, they managed the whole journey with no back-up or support vehicles, descending down the length of Africa – and of course crossing the Sahara – and even managing the whole journey without a compass, an achievement of truly epic proportions!

The places that your bike will take you are a million miles from the socially secure cocoon offered by our modern comforts of life – and, perhaps more importantly, distant from the mechanical comfort and safety that access to a main dealer represents. These days we have unsurpassed levels of technology going into modern motorcycles, technology that works consistently and dependably, but a super-efficient engine management system will not fix a puncture or change your brake pads for you. Remember the definition. When you are overlanding – in the proper sense – you are self-reliant. Your success, and therefore your objective, depends entirely upon your own ability to solve any problems you might encounter along the way. Not all of us are fortunate enough to have natural mechanical talent. Indeed, there are some who have never wielded a spanner in anger, preferring to 'leave it to the dealer', but for them what might be the journey of a lifetime could easily be ruined for want of a small kernel of knowledge – knowing how to resolve a problem that has just stopped you in your tracks.

Those intrepid voyagers of the Thirties endured challenges beyond those that most of us could ever imagine, but it was also inevitable that they would face the mechanical challenges of keeping their machines running properly. Without dealer support or diagnostic computers, their progress was maintained by nothing more than their own knowledge and resourcefulness, plus a handful of simple tools. By today's standards, their skills might seem basic, but they were enough to keep them moving, enough to get them out of trouble and onwards to their destination. These days, though, things are a little different. Reliable electrical systems, engine management computers and advanced manufacturing processes have made major breakdowns almost a thing of the past, leading a lot of motorcycle owners into complacency, with many leaving even simple repairs to be done by a main dealer. But this has also created a void in the mechanical knowledge of the average motorcyclist, and it is exactly this void I hope to be able to help you fill.

Thankfully there is no magic involved in maintenance. All is possible with some thought, preparation and a little help from someone who knows how to spin a spanner or two.

So, what are we waiting for? Grab some tools and let's go and get our hands dirty!

Enjoy the read!

Greg Baker
October 2012

← **The author discusses the finer points of KTM's fuelling system with the locals deep in Morocco.**
📷 Robert Wicks

The motorcyclist's workshop is a truly multi-functional space and can provide a multitude of facilities for the user. Its flexibility can be endless, providing a workspace, a storage area, even a haven of peace and tranquillity, giving you a place for reflection, for inspiration and for planning the next adventure! Its primary function, though, is to be a place where a motorcycle can be repaired or prepared for use. While it does not necessarily need to be large, you do need enough room to move. With careful planning, effective use of space and a couple of specialist accessories, your workshop can become a place where you will be able to perform virtually every job you are likely to need to do on your motorcycle.

How big does it need to be? How long is a piece of string? Although life experience tells us that bigger is always better, what we can say is that you have to make the best of what you have, as few of us have the luxury of being able to create a totally new and bespoke space. The size of your garage is generally determined by the age of your house – the older the house, the smaller the typical family car of the day would have been and the garage will be correspondingly sized. An older house might have a garage as small as 16ft x 8ft (4.8m x 2.4m) but most contemporary dwellings will have something around 10ft x 20ft (3m x 6m), which will be large enough to accommodate a family-sized car.

The challenge comes in making the best of your working space. A large adventure bike with luggage could be over 3ft wide and if it's parked in the middle of an 8ft garage there will only be 2ft 6in left on each side – clearly working in this space is something that has to be planned! Making the most effective use of your space is the key to success here, and with a little imagination and an accessory or two you will be able to create a comfortable and effective workspace that will pay dividends in the long run.

↑ Make your garage a pleasant place to be as you will likely spend a lot of time in there.

📷 Author

The workshop is a pivotal area for anyone who is preparing for a tour, or who wants simply to look after their own bike. We will discover how, with a little work, even a relatively small space can be transformed into a comfortable and effective workspace. Defining what you want to achieve in your workshop is important, as it will have a significant impact on the way that your working area is set out. Will you be storing the bike there? Will you be keeping the car in there too? Clearly many decisions have to be made fairly early on about layout, but all of these factors will influence the end result.

First and foremost, though, it is a place for work to be done, from a simple oil change or removing a wheel to a full engine stripdown. Your area must allow you to perform tasks related to the motorcycle, store the bike and its accessories, your tools and perhaps also – depending on your family dynamic – be a place for bicycles, skateboards and a washing machine.

First steps

If you are lucky enough to be able to start with a completely empty space, take a few moments to visualise what you will be doing in there and how you will be using the space. Put the bike in the middle of the floor and imagine where you would put a workbench, or perhaps where your tools will be stored. It is surprising how many of your first and immediate thoughts will actually translate into the final design and layout of your workshop.

Are there any windows or access doors? Windows let in useful natural light, and if there is one at the back of the garage it makes a perfect place to put a workbench. Side windows are good for ventilation (if they open!) and great for natural light, but it is not so good to place benches next to them as a lot of valuable floor space will be taken up.

Having a side door can be a great advantage, but it can sometimes work against you too. A side door allows you to secure the main front doors from the inside, making it harder for anyone to gain unauthorised access, but a side door that opens *into* the garage can compromise storage space as well as reducing the opportunities for placing workbenches.

If you are forced to accommodate other more domestic items in your workshop area, then maybe you could consider creating a partition to separate the two, with perhaps a separate 'utility' area for the house as well as the workshop area for yourself. This is actually a good solution, giving you another wall for shelving or cabinets, and a physical separation of domestic clutter from the important stuff in your workshop.

Security

It is inevitable that over time the value of the contents of your garage or workshop will increase – sometimes it can be quite an eye-opener to count up exactly how much you have spent! Unfortunately, the high value and relative portability of these items make them very attractive to the determined thief, and a poorly secured workshop or garage can be very quickly emptied of anything of value. Thankfully a few simple steps can make life a lot less simple for those thinking of relieving us of our 'treasures'.

The conventional 'up-and-over' door is notoriously easy to open even when locked shut, but you can increase its security by fitting devices to prevent this. If you have an alternative access door, the main door can be locked from the inside with shoot bolts or similar. If you do not have another access point, the main doors can be locked from the outside with hasps and padlocks, but they must be fitted to each bottom corner to prevent the door being 'peeled' open. If any fasteners or fixings are on the outside of the door, use one-way security screws or dome-headed carriage bolts which can not be unscrewed from the outside. Fit a quality security hasp and secure it to the doorframe in such a way that the door itself conceals the fasteners. It might seem obvious, but do not rely on a cheap lock for your security – you might have thousands of pounds tied up in tools and machinery inside your workshop so it makes sense to protect it with a security-rated padlock.

- Traditional wooden doors should have at least one domed carriage bolt on each part of the hinge to prevent them being unscrewed from the frame and simply lifted off. Again, a good-quality locking hasp must be fitted using security screws or carriage bolts. On a wooden door, however, it is wise to reinforce this with a steel backing plate which will help prevent it being prised off with a crowbar.
- Keep your doors closed when working in your garage to prevent prying eyes looking in and seeing what you have in there. Villains will quite often cruise around in vans looking for their next target – they will not need a second invitation to come back after dark to take a closer look!
- Most theft is opportunistic, and takes place very quickly, so your security measures should not end at the main door. The longer a thief is at his job the more likely he is to be caught, so do not make it easy for him.
- Secure larger pieces of equipment with a cable and lock through handles.
- If possible, tool chests and cabinets should be kept locked when not in use.
- If you secure your bike with a lock and chain, make sure the chain is kept up off the floor as this makes attacking it with bolt-croppers or a grinder twice as hard.
- If possible install a ground anchor close to a wall – having the chain between the bike and a wall makes it much harder to attack.

← **Bigger is nearly always better where security is concerned.**
📷 Author

← **Keeping the chain off the floor makes it harder to attack.**
📷 Haynes

- If your house is protected by a burglar alarm, extend its protection to your workshop too.
- Security lighting is a cheap way to remove a thief's cover of darkness.

Layout

Designing the layout of your workshop might initially seem quite simple, but it is not always so straightforward when you take into consideration the various elements you need to accommodate. There is nothing 'small scale' about a modern adventure motorcycle, and there may eventually be some large and heavy pieces of equipment which you will need to use and store. Inevitably your space requirements will increase along with your skill and ability levels, so some consideration should really be given to future expansion. Some elements of your design will be fixed at an early stage; heavy workbenches, fixed cupboards and fitted lighting are some examples, but other items such as tool cabinets are more flexible and can be placed almost anywhere they are needed. Our ultimate aim, though, is to give our workshop as much floor space as possible, and this will probably mean taking advantage of fixing cupboards over workbenches, and creating thin storage modules which have a small footprint. All of these strategies will help achieve your objective.

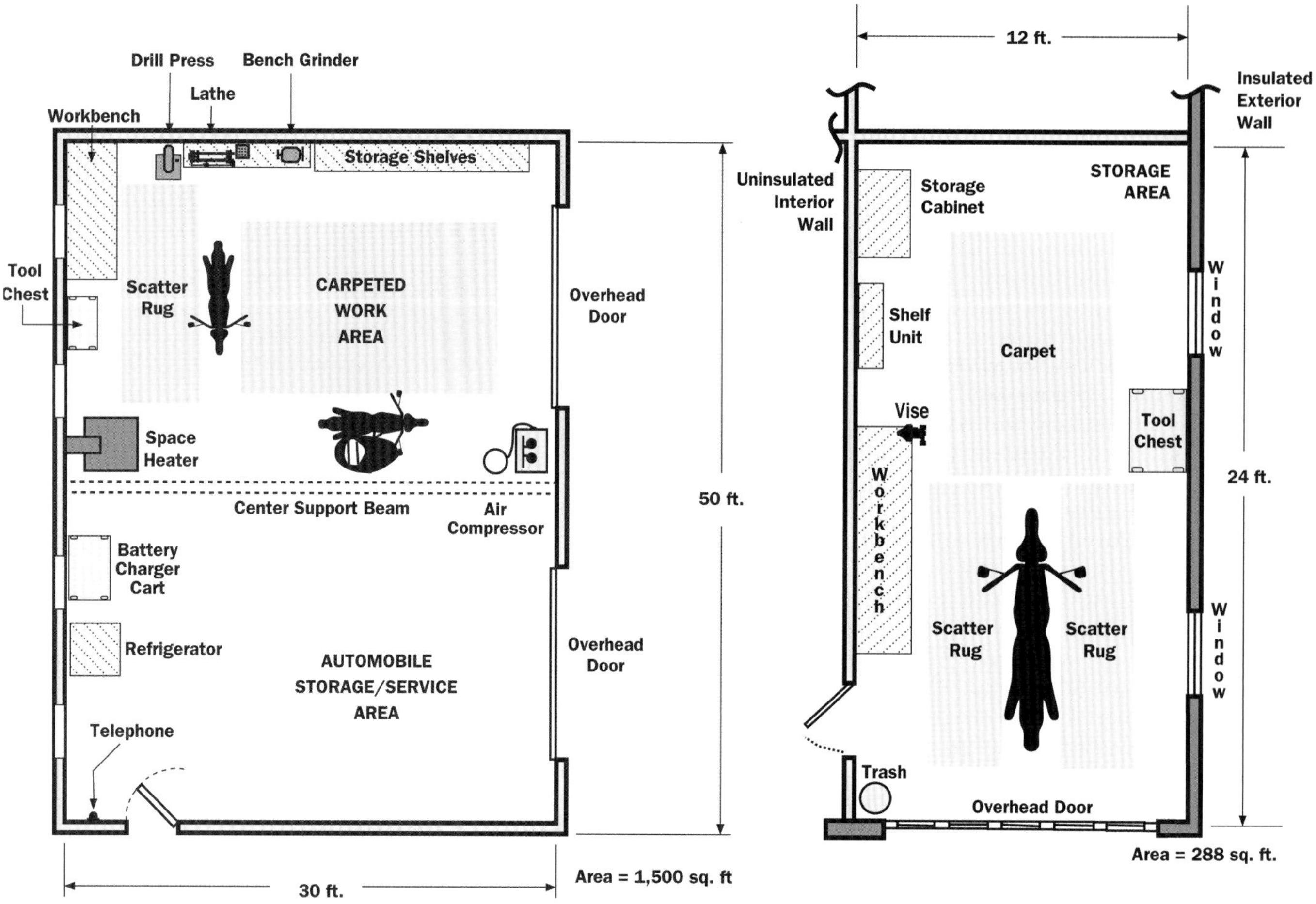
Drill Press
Bench Grinder
Lathe
Workbench
Storage Shelves
Tool Chest
Scatter Rug
CARPETED WORK AREA
Overhead Door
Space Heater
Center Support Beam
Air Compressor
50 ft.
Battery Charger Cart
Refrigerator
AUTOMOBILE STORAGE/SERVICE AREA
Overhead Door
Telephone
30 ft.
Area = 1,500 sq. ft
12 ft.
Insulated Exterior Wall
Uninsulated Interior Wall
Storage Cabinet
STORAGE AREA
Window
Shelf Unit
Carpet
Vise
Tool Chest
24 ft.
Workbench
Scatter Rug
Scatter Rug
Window
Trash
Overhead Door
Area = 288 sq. ft.

↑ A couple of ideal workshop layouts.
Charlie Masi – Whitehorse Press

One simple way of making a workshop more efficient is to keep things to hand. When you begin working, you will soon get an idea of which tools will be needed the most. Clearly, frequently used items need to be more accessible than the others, and should be stored accordingly.

Some jobs you do will be messier than others and designating 'dirty' and 'clean' areas of your workspace is a good practice, and allows you to separate many aspects of your maintenance. A good example of this is having one bench for your electrical work and another for engine work. This kind of segregation allows you to keep appropriate tools close to hand too.

Adequate supply points are essential, for example having electrical sockets on both sides of the garage avoids using extension leads. If you have a compressor try to keep it close to the main door so that the hose will reach far enough for you to be able to use it outside.

The principal factors that will ultimately determine your workshop layout are:

- Power supplies
- Lighting
- Work surfaces
- Storage
- Tools and equipment

Power supplies

In everything but the most basic and temporary workshop, a power supply is essential. Without an electrical supply you have little opportunity for lighting or using any power tools or accessories. While not ideal, smaller appliances such as lead lights, hand drills and grinders can be used with a properly rated extension cable, but in every case you must be sure that all the cable is fully deployed from the reel to prevent it becoming overheated. Larger and more current heavy tools such as welders or compressors will require a fixed power outlet because very few extension cables will have the capacity to deliver the continuous high current required by these devices.

If you are able to start from scratch, you can design your electrical supply layout to suit your exact needs, but remember that it is rarely worth scrimping on power sockets so always fit double outlets wherever you can. Think about placing your power outlets where they will be most useful and set your light switches where they can be operated as you enter or leave the workshop. Workbenches should also have their own power supply, and often it will be beneficial to have a supply at each end of the bench to avoid having cables trailing over your workspace.

The best placement for a power socket on an open or

bare wall will be about halfway between floor and ceiling, making it easily accessible for most functions. Any power outlet sockets or switches, and any cable trunking or conduits should ideally be rated for industrial use and be heavy-duty metal-cased units. Light-duty plastic domestic sockets may simply not be durable or resilient enough to withstand the inevitable knocks and bumps of the workshop. Providing a power supply on an outside wall is often overlooked, but having one allows you to use your tools outside without the inconvenience of a trailing cable. In this case, however, it is absolutely vital that a correctly rated and weatherproof unit is used.

Ensure your power supply is adequately protected with a correctly fitted and installed consumer unit, and preferably independent of the supply to your house – if you trip a circuit in the garage it should not plunge the rest of the house into darkness! All circuits should be protected by appropriate devices such as RCD (residual current device) circuit breakers.

Before you embark upon any electrical work or modification please be mindful that any mistake with or misuse of mains electricity can have fatal results, and local regulations might actually prohibit installation or modification of domestic electrical circuits by anyone other than a certified electrical engineer. Always consult an approved supplier who is qualified to perform work or checks to ensure the safety and integrity of the electrical supply, and that all work complies with any applicable local safety standards.

Lighting

Using the correct type of lighting is essential, as there is nothing worse than trying to do a complex and fiddly job if the lighting is poor or dim. The best tools in the world are no good unless you can see what you are doing with them!

Fluorescent lighting is without doubt the best source of light in the workshop, as it gives very flat illumination with minimal shadows. The units used should ideally have shrouding of some kind both to protect the tube from damage and also to contain it in case it is damaged. High-wattage tubes produce more light, but equally important is the 'colour temperature' of the tube itself. Some tubes give a warm yellow light (4,300k) while others give a more blue light (5,600k) that is closer to natural light, which is much easier to work in. The latest generation of fluorescent lighting uses high-tech ballast units which operate at much higher frequencies than older equipment, giving a much quicker start-up and almost completely eliminating flicker.

Plan the placement of your main workspace lighting carefully to give the best and most effective spread of light. If using fluorescent tubes, two rows will illuminate both sides of the bike without leaving any shadowed areas.

Workbenches should be particularly well lit as it is likely that some jobs will involve small parts or complex assemblies. Doing an intricate job with poor lighting increases your chance of component loss, failure – and frustration! Even using a simple desk lamp can make all the difference to the ease with which a job can be achieved. If possible this should be supplemented with a more even and diffuse light

⬋ This looks like a disaster waiting to happen!
📷 Author

⬇ This is how it should be done.
📷 Author

source. If you have a shelf above the workbench, a small tubular lamp can be easily affixed to its underside and will give a very useful spread of light.

A hand-held LED inspection light is always useful for lighting awkward nooks and crannies, and using a head torch leaves both hands free for those particularly fiddly jobs. Likewise, keep a small 'pencil' torch handy to be able to peer into the darkest corners of your bike!

Work surfaces

A good bench is an essential and central item in any workshop, and the place where most of your tasks will be performed. Various solutions are available, with many DIY and tool retailers listing a variety of products which will suit most needs. Beware of the cheaper options, though, because they will invariably be constructed using lighter-grade materials and may not be able to withstand some of the 'heavier' uses they may be subjected to. A home-built bench may offer the best solution in some circumstances, giving you the flexibility to use an otherwise awkward corner. A quick browse on the internet should give you more than enough inspiration! If you plan on doing much engine work, or anything oily or greasy, then think about having a steel-topped bench which will be far more sturdy and durable

than a wooden or MDF surface and certainly easier to keep clean. On the other hand, a smooth laminated surface is ideal for clean tasks such as electrical work.

Storage

Storage is a commodity that always seems in short supply. From tools to equipment, riding gear and boots, almost everything you use in the course of riding a motorcycle will require storage. Obviously, how and where you store things depends entirely on what they are. Large and heavy pieces of equipment like compressors and jacks will probably always stay on the floor, but they can also be stowed underneath a bench to save floor space. Hand tools such as socket sets and spanners are ideally stored in a tool-chest which will allow you to organise your tools and keep them close to where they are needed. Some chests are fitted with castors so that they can be easily moved around the workshop, and also double as a handy seat when working on the bike. A tall steel cabinet with adjustable shelves is very useful for stowing medium-sized hand tools such as electric drills or any other DIY items, and if it is lockable its top shelf is probably the best place to store any hazardous chemicals or products.

Often overlooked is the need to store your riding gear properly. A typical motorcycle jacket is quite bulky, and a full overlanding suit is bulkier still, but there will very often be other items of kit to consider, such as a lightweight summer jacket and trousers, an oversuit and, of course, your helmet, boots and gloves! It is essential to store these items properly to keep them in tip-top condition and ready to use. There is nothing worse than reaching for your helmet or gloves only to find that they are either smelly or have even become mouldy from being stowed in a dark, damp environment. Try to keep your kit on hangers as these help preserve a garment's shape and hold it open so any absorbed moisture from perspiration can dry out. If you store kit in a cabinet or cupboard, ensure that it is well ventilated and allows good airflow. This is where a dehumidifier can bring benefits to your garage. Even a small unit can have an extraction rate of up to 10 litres of moisture per day, ensuring a good dry atmosphere in your workshop which will help keep your bike and your tools rust-free.

When considering your storage requirements, try to build in a space for your bike's accessories. Panniers are a classic example as they are bulky and quite often empty, and if left on the bike can increase fuel consumption dramatically. Other items such as tank-bags, spare windshields and hand-guards are all demountable and often only used occasionally, which means that they need storing when not on the bike.

Workshop safety

Safety in the workshop is of paramount importance, especially if you are working in a smallish space. Keep the floor free from trip hazards like cables or hoses wherever possible; and if you are already working in a small area, do not make it any smaller by leaving things on the floor. There is nothing more disheartening than stepping back to admire your work, but actually treading on and breaking a body panel – it has happened and it is painful!

Workshop tools and equipment will invariably be quite powerful, and can cause a lot of damage or injury if not used properly. Be sure to follow the manufacturer's instructions for commissioning and using apparatus. Remember, if you think it might not be safe to use, then it probably is not.

Fire is a permanent hazard in the workshop, and the risk is magnified if you find yourself working on the fuel system or carburettor. Always keep an appropriate fire extinguisher close to hand and in a place where it can be reached easily in a hurry. Dry powder or CO_2 extinguishers must be used instead of water or foam extinguishers, which have their own risks if used in an electrical environment. These are readily available from most DIY outlets these days, and are cheap compared to the cost of loss or damage that a fire might cause. Fix one by each doorway or access point.

↑ The perfect way to keep your kit in good shape.
📷 Bikertidy.co.uk

Spillage of any fluid should be attended to without delay. Take care that you adopt the correct approach to whatever has been spilled. Oil and other non-volatile fluids can be soaked up with a handful of sawdust or even cat litter, which can be swept up to leave very little contaminant behind. Fuel or any other solvents should be mopped up with a cloth or a handful of rags which should immediately be put outside the workshop to allow the vapours to disperse safely in the atmosphere. If the spillage is significant the doors must be left open for a good 10–15 minutes to allow any volatile gases to be purged and disperse into the outside atmosphere.

Use appropriate and approved containers for storing fuel, or other dangerous fluids. Old engine oil or any other unwanted hydrocarbon products should be drained into an appropriate can or suitable container and disposed of at your nearest recycling centre. Do not pour it onto the ground or empty it into a drainage system. Remember also that old soft drinks bottles should never be used to store dangerous fluids.

← The right fire extinguisher is essential in any workshop.
📷 Author

Personal safety

There are many hazards that you will encounter in your workshop, some obvious, others not. One of the best things you can do is have a good first aid kit in a prominent and easily accessible position. Keep it well stocked and replace any items that you use or that might have a 'best before' expiry date.

Always wear eye protection in the form of goggles or safety spectacles when using any kind of power tool that might produce sparks, chips, dust or swarf. Virtually any eye injury will be extremely painful as well as taking a long time to heal, so to risk losing or impairing your vision by not taking a simple protective precaution like using goggles or safety glasses is pure folly.

An overall or boiler suit will protect your clothing and will keep you warmer on cool days, while the use of safety boots or shoes will protect your feet. Trainers have negligible value in this respect.

Keep a good supply of surgical rubber or PVC gloves to use when performing operations that involve contact with oils or greases. These not only reduce the risk to your skin of contact dermatitis, but will also make it a lot easier to keep yourself clean, especially when dealing with dirty components like drive chains.

If you are performing any operation which produces fine dust or you are using spray paint cans or full spraying equipment, an appropriate respiration mask is vital. This is especially important if you are working on any braking components as brake dust can contain particles of asbestos.

Various types are available, from a simple dust mask to a full multi-stage canister filter – use the best one to suit your needs.

Many of the chemicals and products used in motorcycle maintenance can be noxious, so ensure your working space has adequate ventilation, and always leave an outside door open if you are using solvents or similar. Never use volatile fluids in a closed, confined space as the effects from inhaling solvent vapours can cause disorientation, dizziness and confusion. Never be tempted to run your engine in a closed garage – the carbon monoxide in the exhaust fumes is extremely toxic and can cause the rapid onset of gas poisoning.

Earplugs are also simple items that should be considered as important in the workshop as they are while riding the bike. Some power tool operations like grinding or pneumatic chiselling can produce very high levels of noise at the frequencies that are most damaging to hearing.

Always make sure that your bike is secure when you are working on it. Check it for balance when removing wheels as some models require an additional prop under the sump to prevent them tipping forwards. If the bike is on a ramp or a bench, use a pair of ratchet tie-down straps to be certain it can not topple sideways. If you have a high-torque fastener to remove, such as a rear wheel spindle nut or a final drive sprocket nut, always try to have an assistant to give extra support. Such fasteners should be loosened with the bike on the ground as it is easier than you think to tip a bike over with applied torque, particularly if it is being supported on a paddock stand.

Comfort

Comfort might seem a strange requirement for a workshop, but there are many ways in which being comfortable will improve the quality of the work you are doing.

Unless you are living in the tropics, some form of heating will be essential in the workshop, especially if you are in a colder climate. Physical work can become difficult if the temperature around you drops too low and your fingers get cold, or it can be made cumbersome by the need to wear additional clothing or gloves, so even a small heater can make a huge difference in these conditions. Electrical heating is generally most convenient to use, although any more than very occasional use will require a properly rated domestic electrical supply rather than an extension cable, and can also be less effective for larger open areas. Heating systems requiring bottled gas cannot be recommended due to the risk posed by fuel vapour that may be present.

Clearly heating an area like a workshop or garage is going to be quite expensive, more so if the space is in regular use. Insulation will make a tremendous difference to costs, and it is relatively simple to achieve, especially as your workshop will usually be of a very basic construction, with single-skin brick walls and a simple felted ply or chipboard roof. If it is possible

→ ↓ First aid is not always just about sticking plasters!
📷 Author

to insulate both the walls and the roof, huge benefits can be had in both keeping your space warm and fuel costs low.

The floor of the workshop is often overlooked and can have its own set of implications for the way you work. In a typical garage the floor will be a rough-cast concrete, laid without a great deal of care as to it being smooth or flat. Very often it will have a very rough surface and frequently will be chemically unstable, which in simple terms means that the surface loses its structural integrity and starts to release lots of dust, or in the worst cases completely breaks up and cracks. A dusty floor can be treated with a stabilising solution which will re-bond the loose surface, then given a coat or two of a proprietary floor paint that will give a long-lasting and very durable finish. A cracked or broken floor will need more work to put right, necessitating filling any holes or cracks and restoring a flat surface with an epoxy 'self-levelling' compound. If your budget will stretch a little further, look at installing interlocking PVC tiles which give a flat and secure surface that is also very durable and easy to keep clean.

On any floor, however, using a couple of carpet off-cuts or an old rug can be of great benefit in keeping your feet warm while standing. Using a small kneeling pad is a lot kinder on the knees, but it might be better to use a small stool for those low-down jobs on the bike – this will save your knees and ankles in the long term, and prevent 'pins and needles' when you eventually stand up again!

Garage equipment

There are endless possibilities for equipping your workshop. Indeed, you could spend a small fortune on a lot of stuff that you will probably never use, so it is better to spend your money wisely on a few essentials first, then build your asset list as you go along. Concentrate on buying the kit you are actually going to use rather than stuff you *think* you may use.

An air compressor is perhaps one of the most versatile pieces of equipment you can invest in, but it is not always just about inflating tyres. Compressed air can be used to drive hand tools such as grinders, sanders and, of course, the ubiquitous 'windy gun' for impact-driving sockets. It will drive a reciprocating saw, a pneumatic chisel or even a needle belt sander in confined spaces. A concentrated blast of compressed air will clear most blockages in a carburettor, and when used in a blasting cabinet can clean and restore aluminium finishes.

If you are going to be doing a lot of work on your motorcycle, then some means of getting the bike up off the floor will be a godsend. Raising the bike like this makes doing almost any task so much simpler, especially if it avoids you lying or kneeling on the floor. A hydraulic lift is the ideal solution here and provides a stable and secure platform upon which to work. Various types are available, according to your budget, from the simple dirt-bike lift which sits under the bike's sump to a full-length bench lift which will

accommodate any bike up to a 350kg cruiser. A paddock stand or similar can be used in conjunction with a hydraulic lift if your bike does not have a centre stand, although it is essential to secure it with supplementary straps. If your roof structure is strong enough, ratchet straps can be used to hold the bike upright, or even serve as a hoist if necessary.

If you are short on space, then a bike mover which is placed under the centre stand or a wheel is a very useful piece of kit, and allows you to manoeuvre the bike around the garage without fighting against a steering lock.

Tools and toolkit

Unfortunately, the first contact with tools that many of you will have is the bike's originally supplied toolkit, and unless it is one of the prestigious early BMW sets it is likely to be sparse and made up of very basic and simple tools, capable of performing only the lightest of jobs. It will be useful for keeping on the bike for an emergency, but do not expect it to be up to the task of performing a home service. To do that you need 'proper' tools rather than cheap items, and while building up a decent toolkit can be a bit of a mission, it is nevertheless hugely rewarding, allowing you to tackle more jobs than you thought! Your toolkit will grow with you, as your skill level and confidence increase, as will the types

↑ **A sturdy bike lift will make most jobs a lot easier to do.**
📷 Author

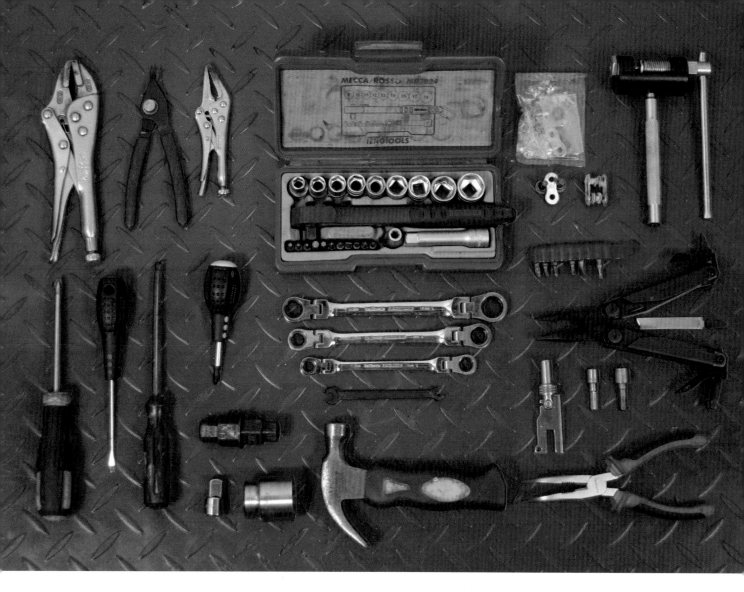

of tool you need to do those more complex jobs. From a simple set of spanners to a single-purpose tool, everything will have a use.

It can be very easy to spend a lot of money on tools, but with a little planning and forethought a comprehensive yet effective set of tools can be created for a modest outlay. One of the first rules to remember is 'You get what you pay for!' The tool market is awash with cheap tool sets of dubious origin, from full socket sets to single screwdrivers, but they are cheap for a reason. Invariably made from inferior materials, poorly finished and inaccurately machined, these tools have little purpose in any toolkit and can often create more problems than they solve. As budget tools are often made from low-grade or inappropriate steel, they can rarely withstand applied forces without deformation or breakage that can result in damage both to the fixing you are trying to remove and to you as the user! At best the tool will break, leaving the fixing unmoved; at worst, however, it can deform and round off the fixing's corners, making it doubly hard to remove later on.

If you know the signs, it can be quite easy to identify a cheaply made tool. Look for poor finishes, flash lines or raised ridges on the handles and steer very clear of anything that is unbranded. Very often the packaging or storage case

will tell a tale too. Check the latches of a socket set's case, making sure that they are substantial enough to stay securely closed and perhaps locked. Check the hinges as well – a thermoformed plastic case can fatigue after time, leading to cracking and failure of the hinge. The inner storage tray needs to be substantial enough to hold the sockets safely inside the case for the life of the kit – many of the cheaper sets will only have a flimsy vacuum-formed plastic insert that will crack and break after very little use, leaving your sockets in disarray.

Quality tools have a certain look and feel to them. When choosing a tool, take a close look at it, checking the quality of its finish. If it is plated, is it a bright silvery chrome or a more yellow nickel plate? A quality chrome plating will be deep and polished to a lustrous finish while a cheaper, thinner plating will be more obvious. Nickel plating tends to be more durable and work resistant. The disadvantage of plated tools is that the plating can become separated from the base metal. If the plating is thick it can present sharp edges which could be dangerous to the user, while thin plating will simply peel or rub off allowing the base metal to corrode.

The same rules apply to selecting the best spanners you can afford. The really cheap ones will be crudely forged, with thin cosmetic chrome plating over rough flash lines and coarse grinding marks. These really are the ones to avoid! Quality spanners will have been well forged in the first place, avoiding the need for a lot of finish grinding. There will be no flash marks or seams along the shaft, and they will be either shot-peened or plated. Shot-peening gives a dull satin finish and alters the metallurgy of the outer layers of the steel, making it stronger and more resistant to corrosion. Deep chroming is a cosmetic treatment, giving the tool a good finish and making it easy to keep clean.

Give yourself an idea of what the tool will feel like when you are using it: a good-quality tool will feel 'right' when held in your hand. Generally tools will have either a plated, polished or blasted finish, and they will be presented in a good quality case that has been designed to last as long as the tools it carries. Look for signs that the work surfaces of the tools have been ground or machined to size, for example the inner faces of an open-ended spanner must be accurate to their declared size and, of course, perfectly parallel. Ratcheting socket drivers should ideally have a nice smooth action, with a fine ratchet – too coarse and it might be difficult to rotate in a confined space. Larger socket drivers usually have 40 click ratchets, while smaller drivers can have more flexibility at up to 72 clicks per 360° rotation, but they cannot deliver the same levels of tightening torque.

Every fastener on your motorcycle will have been tightened by a very specific amount that will be dependent upon the type of fastener and the material it is made of, as well as the material it is being fastened into. One of the more essential items in your home toolkit, therefore, will be a torque wrench.

WHAT IS TORQUE?

In a nutshell, torque can be loosely described as 'rotational force' or the force you put into something to make it turn. In other words, as you pull harder on a spanner to tighten a nut, you apply more torque to the fastener. Modern manufacturing techniques have enabled the production of precisely engineered components using extremely light materials, and very often these materials can be damaged or distorted by using too much force. Using a torque wrench allows the application of a very precise amount of rotational force to a fastener to ensure that it remains in place without overtightening it, which would risk damaging either the fastener or, more likely, the casting it is being screwed into.

A good example of this would be engine casings, which rely greatly upon all the bolts being fastened to the same degree, allowing the casing to stay flat and preventing any oil leaks. Torque is also used to ensure that a fastener cannot loosen, an example being the clamps used to hold handlebars or gear levers.

A very useful exercise to perform is setting a variety of fasteners with a torque wrench, then using an ordinary spanner or socket driver to loosen and retighten them, before rechecking them with a torque wrench. It can be surprising just how little force is required to secure nuts and bolts, especially in the case of many smaller fasteners.

← Using a torque wrench ensures accurate and consistent tightening.
📷 Haynes

t is fair to say that today's motorcycles are probably among the
most reliable machines ever made. There are some exceptions,
of course, but in the main the technological advances such as
computer-controlled engine management systems, electronic fuel
injection and CAN-bus electrical systems have made significant
breakdowns virtually a thing of the past. Many of these systems
have been developed by manufacturers specifically for their
particular models, and their complexity often renders them
inaccessible to all but authorised dealers who have the necessary
diagnostic reading equipment.

Luckily these systems have an inherently high reliability rate
and in the main will give many years of service without any
problem. These control systems also have the advantage of
being highly flexible as they can be reprogrammed to control the
various parameters of engine management. For example, the
fuelling map (the programme that controls fuel delivery into the
engine) can be reprogrammed to allow the engine to run on the
lower-octane fuel that is found in many third world countries.

Understandably, these control systems are critically important
to the effective and efficient running of the engine, and as many
of the engine management parameters are linked it is usual
that only an authorised dealer with access to the appropriate
equipment will be able to read or re-programme the system.
There might be the occasional need for a re-map or a firmware
upgrade to adjust, for example, an ignition parameter which will
be uploaded to the motorcycle's ECU (engine control unit) with
the dealer's diagnostic computer. This will generally be done as
part of a dealer service, but if there is a minor glitch it can often
be resolved with a 'soft' reset, achieved by simply turning off the
ignition and restarting the engine.

Although it is a machine, a motorcycle can be seen to have some very organic requirements. It needs feeding, it needs welfare, it needs love and care from you – in essence, you almost become its parent. Satisfy these basic needs and the bike will be able to give you everything of which it is capable. However, neglect any of these aspects of its care and you run the risk of something not working properly or failing completely, causing a breakdown. The most obvious item is, of course, fuel. If you run out of fuel the bike stops – but how many of us know how far we can go on a full tank? Less obvious is engine lubrication. It can be very easy to forget to check the oil level of your bike, but by the time you notice that it is low, or even worse when you hear a strange noise, then the damage has probably already been done. Component failure may not always be imminent, but oil starvation significantly shortens bearing life and accelerates mechanical wear. It is also completely avoidable!

A bike's reliability is completely dependent upon the foundations of basic maintenance, but paradoxically it is that reliability that can become an inherent contribution to a longer-term problem. Being disciplined against complacency and getting into the habit of making a few basic checks each time you ride will allow you to see a problem and resolve it by reacting to the symptoms rather than needing to repair a component failure. Having a basic knowledge of your bike and what is needed to keep it running will give you a much better insight into how the various parts work, and how they integrate with each other to become the motorcycle that we sometimes take for granted. By being aware of the way your motorcycle runs when it is 'well' will also mean that you will also be more attuned to any problems that arise – in short, look after your bike and it will look after you.

Oil and lubrication

An engine's oil is its lifeblood. It lubricates, it cools and it cleans almost every component in the engine, from the heat of the pistons and combustion chamber to the smallest and most inaccessible parts of the engine. Yet despite it performing a crucially important task, it is often overlooked and taken for granted. Undoubtedly, the biggest part of its job is lubrication, providing a thin yet resilient film of protection between the metal surfaces of the engine which bear against each other, minimising friction and reducing wear to a negligible amount. To do this properly, the oil has to be pumped at high pressure through a complex and convoluted circuit to be delivered to the exact places where it is needed.

To achieve this, the oil has to have many properties and characteristics. It needs to be thin enough to flow easily round the lubrication circuit when the engine is cold, but it also has to remain thick enough to provide good protection when the engine is hot, as well as leaving a residual oil film when the engine is not running. Although it might appear to be relatively simple, oil is in reality an incredibly complex product both in physical and chemical terms.

As the oil does its job it gathers up contaminants and debris along the way. It will absorb many of the chemical by-products of the combustion process as well as picking up any unburned fuel, partially burned hydrocarbons, atmospheric dirt, metal wear particles and blow-by carbon particles. Chemical and gaseous contaminants will generally be released as the oil is depressurised within the crankcase where the resulting vapour is recirculated via a breather into the air filter chamber and reintroduced into the combustion cycle. Larger particles need to be removed from the oil to prevent them from causing wear or, in the worst case, clogging the slender oilways and starving the engine of lubrication.

To achieve this the oil must be passed through a filter. There are various ways to do this, but the most common is the use of a spin-on cartridge filter. A typical filter will have two media types: primary and secondary. The primary medium can stop particles as small as 25–30 microns (human hair is 65–70 microns in size) and the secondary medium can stop particles as small as 5–10 microns. 'Full-flow' filters should be avoided as they generally utilise primary media alone, giving high flow rates at the cost of lower filtration levels. Low-end or cheap filters will invariably have media that allow larger particles to pass through, again reducing filtering efficiency and potentially allowing high wear rates. Oil filters tend to be relatively easy to change and will have a bypass valve which will allow an emergency flow of oil to continue should the filter become blocked or clogged.

Contaminants that are too small to be collected by the filter will continue to circulate with the oil and will be removed only when the oil is changed. In the longer term, some contaminants will drop out of the oil and fall to the bottom of the sump where, over time, they consolidate to form a nasty black sludge. This sludge will generally do no harm if left undisturbed, and can be extracted if ever the sump is removed. Do not worry too much as the oil gets darker with age – it is just doing its job!

There are many different oils available on the market and every one will claim to be better at something than its rivals. The bewildering amount of information available about engine oil, and the different opinions and arguments that occur whenever oil is discussed, are bound to create a degree of confusion.

↓ **The oil works hard at every stage of its journey through the engine.**
📷 Author

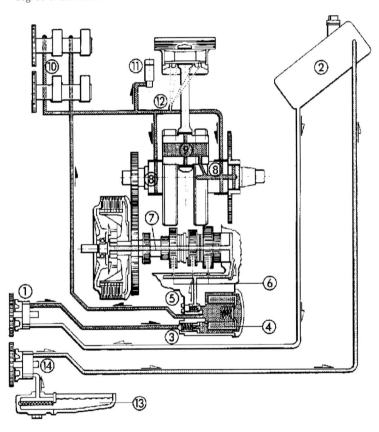

← **For maximum protection, replace the filter at each oil change.**
📷 Author

OIL SPECIFICATIONS AND TYPES AT A GLANCE

There are many different brands of oil available in the marketplace, and each manufacturer seems to adopt a different standard to classify its products. Unfortunately, there is not one *consistent* standard that is used across the board.

The first rule of thumb should be to use the recommended oils as specified in your bike's owners' manual wherever possible. However, the world is not perfect, and sometimes you may have to use an alternative. Being able to decipher some of the markings on the can will help you make a choice.

JASO – Japanese Automotive Standards Organisation

Created to identify and implement regulation in the standards of lubrication required by the Japanese automotive industry, JASO introduced a basic identifier to separate oils intended for use in motorcycles and cars.

MA Oil without friction modifiers which is suitable for use with wet-clutch systems.

MB Oil with friction modifiers which is *not* suitable for wet-clutch systems, as it will make the clutch slip.

API – American Petroleum Institute

As engine technology develops, the level of protection required also increases. API classifies oil with letters according to the level of protection. The further into the alphabet, the higher the protection offered. Prefixes starting 'S' indicate that the oil is intended for use in petrol engines, and 'C' designates diesel engine usage.

SJ Suitable for 2001 and older engines.

SL Suitable for 2004 and older engines.

SM Suitable for 2010 and older engines.

SN Suitable for 2011 and older vehicles (introduced in October 2010): designed to provide improved high-temperature deposit protection for pistons, more stringent sludge control, improved fuel economy, emission control system compatibility, and protection of engines operating on ethanol-containing fuels up to E85.

SAE – Society of Automotive Engineers

This is possibly the most recognised oil standard. SAE stands for the Society of Automotive Engineers, based in the USA. The SAE grade specifies the oil's viscosity, or the 'thickness' of the oil – the lower the number, the 'thinner' the oil; thus SAE 30 is less viscous than SAE 40. Multigrade oils combine these numbers to show their viscosities at both high and low temperatures. The viscosity of all oils falls as they get hot – and multi-grade oils are formulated to minimise this effect.

Multi-grade oils are defined by a viscosity rating at a low temperature, as well as one at 100°C. In simple terms a multi-grade oil will give the same levels of protection over a range of ambient temperatures. However, older engines with greater operating tolerances may require a thicker oil to give the required level of protection, so using a super-efficient oil designed for a modern engine may not protect it as well as the 'old-school' product!

SAE 20w/50
Ambient temperature range: –10°C to 40°C

SAE 10w/40
Ambient temperature range: –20°C to 40°C

SAE 05w/50
Ambient temperature range: –30°C to 40°C

SAE 00w/50
Ambient temperature range: –40°C to 40°C

ACEA – Association des Constructeurs Européens d'Automobiles

(European Automobile Manufacturers' Association) In its complete form the ACEA classification is perhaps the most comprehensive listing of application and suitability. Prefixes beginning with 'A' are for petrol engines, 'B' for passenger car diesel engines, 'C' for catalyst-compatible oils and 'E' for heavy-duty diesel engines. Numerical sub-classifications identify different applications and characteristics.

A1 Low-viscosity, fuel-efficient oil

A2 High-viscosity, standard performance

A3 High-performance and/or extended drain

A5 High-performance, low-viscosity, fuel-efficient oil

Mineral versus synthetic

There will be constant debate about the relative merits of one type of oil over another. Most significant is the difference between mineral and synthetic oils. Without going into too much chemistry, the base mineral oil from which motor oil is derived is produced during the distillation process of crude oil into fuel. This base oil must be treated with various additives and modifiers before it can be used in an engine. Synthetic oil, on the other hand, is a man-made compound of various molecules that are synthesised from simpler chemical compounds. These compounds can be engineered to give very specific performance properties, and they tend to flow more freely at extremely low temperatures and resist breaking down at very high temperatures.

Apart from manufacture, origin and, of course, cost, the significant difference between synthetic oil and mineral oil is in their molecular and particulate structures. The manufacturing process of synthetic oil allows the creation of a very even and uniform molecular structure with precisely defined lubrication characteristics. Conversely, the organic nature of a mineral oil means that its molecular structure is more irregular than that of synthetic oil, but this gives it a real advantage in the early stages of an engine's life.

During the 'running-in' process, the irregular molecular structure of mineral oil lubricates the engine while allowing the uneven surfaces of newly machined components to rub with each other and erode any high spots, making the surfaces even and smooth and completely matched to each other. This is very useful, as the components of the engine gradually wear against each other to give a very fine mating surface. Once this initial 'breaking in' is complete, component wear rates start to decrease, friction levels drop dramatically and oil consumption generally is greatly reduced. This is the point at which you can switch to a synthetic oil and take advantage of the benefits of the 'engineered' protection it can offer.

That said, the motorcycle's manufacturer will have put a great deal of its own research into developing the right oil for its engines, so its recommended specified oil will always be a good choice. Your motorcycle's handbook will contain details of the recommended lubricants to be used, as well as alternative grades that can be used in different climatic conditions. The research and development that goes into creating these lubricants is immense, and very often motorcycle manufacturers will work closely with a lubricant supplier to ensure that the engine will be fully protected at all times. Thankfully, they have done all the hard work so we do not need to worry about much more than making sure the bike's engine is kept topped up with the most suitable oil.

SAE viscosity grades and outdoor temperature range

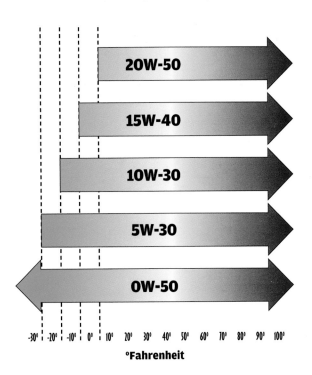

Fully synthetic	Characteristics
0W-30 0W-40 5W-40	■ Fuel economy savings ■ Enhances engine performance and power ■ Ensures engine is protected from wear and deposit build-up ■ Ensures good cold starting and quick circulation in freezing temperatures ■ Gets to moving parts of the engine quickly
Semi-synthetic	
5W-30 10W-40 15W-40	■ Better protection ■ Good protection within the first 10 minutes after starting out ■ Roughly three times better at reducing engine wear ■ Increased intervals between oil changes
Mineral	
10W-40 15W-40	■ Basic protection for a variety of engines ■ Oil needs to be changed more often

Air filters

The air filter is another of those critical components that is hidden away in the depths of the bike and is easy to forget in normal usage. As the name suggests, it is a filter for the air that enters the fuelling system. Without it, dust or other physical particulates in the air would be sucked into the engine with the fuel/air mix and could cause abnormal wear or potential failure. Filters work by trapping any dust or other physical contaminant before it can damage the internal parts of the engine, and when you consider that an engine of 1,000cc displacement running at 4,000rpm will suck something like 1.6 cubic metres of air every minute, you can see why it has to be clean!

The service life of any air filter is determined by the nature of the environment in which the bike is used. In normal urban use an air filter can reasonably be expected to work well for 5–10,000 miles (8–16,000km), but on a dusty desert surface the filter can become clogged after as little as 150 miles (240km). The filter also has to allow air to flow efficiently throughout its life, and leaving it to become too dirty can restrict the volume of air getting into the engine and cause it to run badly, lose power and consume excessive amounts of fuel. Be aware, though, that the opposite can also apply. Manufacturers will set their fuelling or carburation based on the performance of their own approved filter. A sports-type filter with a particularly high airflow rate could possibly affect the fuelling level, which may lead to poor running or, in the worst case, an excessively lean fuel/air mixture creating extremely high combustion temperatures, risking burned valves or a holed piston.

There are three main types of filter; all work using the same principle, but each has its own advantage. With the exception of some competition machines, most modern motorcycles will be supplied with a pleated paper filter. The filter medium we see, however, is a far cry from the papers we come across in everyday life. 'Paper' filter medium is air-permeable, and made from coarse cellulose fibre pulp which is then treated to give it a degree of structural strength. The nature of the fibres and the random way in which they lie create millions of small passages and voids through which the dirty air is drawn. Any particulate contamination in the air is caught and trapped in these voids, allowing clean filtered air to pass into the combustion cycle.

The grade of the filter is determined by the volume and size of the fibres used; a low-volume coarse fibre medium, for instance, will have larger voids which will allow smaller particles through the filter. A higher level of filtration can be obtained using a finer fibre which reduces the size of the voids and will therefore catch smaller particles. As the airflow efficiency of the filter medium is determined by its surface area, pleating the filter paper gives a greater surface area and therefore allows much higher volumes of air into the engine as well as extending service intervals.

Foam filters, which are more often found on off-road or competition bikes, work in a slightly different way from paper filters. These are manufactured using an open-cell polyurethane foam that has been 'wetted' or lightly soaked in a specially formulated oil with a high 'tack' factor. This filter medium gets its high surface area from the thousands of cells in each cubic centimetre. As the air passes through the open cell structure of the foam, any dust particles are caught in the tacky oil in which the foam is coated and clean air passes through into the engine. Foam filters can be a simple, single-density foam, or a dual-stage item with two different grades of foam bonded together to provide a higher level of filtration.

Some filters have a primary stage which is slightly 'hairy' and designed to trap the biggest particles before they clog the main filter. The principal advantage of these filters is that they can easily be cleaned using detergent or a solvent to wash out the contaminants and then re-oiled to restore their efficiency and effectiveness. Some manufacturers offer a supplementary filter 'sock' as an accessory. This is a simple fabric cover for the air filter, designed to capture the largest particles before they get to the main filter. Its simple design means it can easily be removed and shaken clean to restore its performance as a first-stage filter. These socks are designed to be used dry and are particularly useful in extremely dusty conditions.

Cloth and mesh filters are made from layers of fine cotton cloth held between a steel mesh. This composite is then folded and pleated in a similar way to a paper filter to give it a large surface area. The main body of the filter is coated with a high-tack oil similar to that used for foam filters. The absorbent nature of the cotton cloth causes it to swell slightly with the oil, and the gaps in the weave provide the voids to trap dust particles This type of filter combines the best attributes of both paper and foam filters, and it can be washed and re-oiled to restore its performance. There is an on-going debate regarding the effectiveness of this type of filter, however, given the high airflow rates that are often claimed.

Fuel

In many parts of the western world we have not had to worry about fuel grade – or octane – for many years. This is not the case in some parts of the third world where many of the vehicles in daily use do not have the engine technology and developments that we know and take for granted.

New and modern vehicles are simply out of the reach of a vast percentage of the world's population, and the majority of their vehicles are up to 30 years old and kept running by nothing more than necessity and ingenuity. Third-world governments also tend not to place as much importance on environmental protection, and the older vehicles in these countries do not need such sophisticated grades of fuel as our more modern 'clean-burn' engines. As a result, the fuel that is most often produced is the cheapest low-grade fuel possible, with lead compounds still in use rather than the more environmentally friendly but costly additives that are usually found in western fuels.

A modern internal combustion engine is built with efficiency and performance in mind, and this has never been more apparent than with modern motorcycle engines, with some sports models producing power output figures in excess of 200bhp/litre. High cylinder compression ratios, super-efficient gas-flow technology and programmable

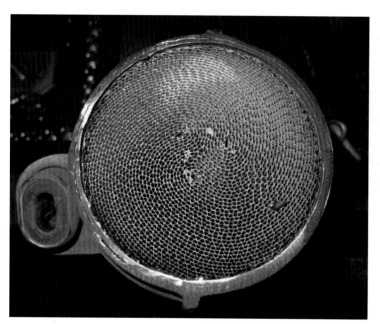

The structure of a catalytic converter is surprisingly delicate.
📷 Author

Catalytic converters

Many years ago concerns for health and the environment led to the removal of the lead compounds that were added to fuel to boost octane and reduce valve face wear, and fuel systems have developed accordingly around this unleaded fuel. Perhaps the most significant recent development in producing a cleaner exhaust has been the catalytic converter or 'cat'.

In simple terms this is a ceramic honeycomb structure (imagine a handful of drinking straws) contained in a separate chamber of the exhaust system that has been given a fine coating of platinum and rhodium. As hot exhaust gases pass through these tubes, they heat the coatings which then react with any remaining hydrocarbon particulate or unburned fuel in the exhaust, converting these gaseous toxins into less harmful compounds such as water and carbon dioxide. However, this reaction will not occur if there is any lead compound present in the fuel. Continued use of leaded fuel will seriously affect the catalytic properties of the unit, ultimately rendering it ineffective and possibly even causing it to become clogged or obstructed. Although one or two tankfuls of leaded will probably not do any harm in the long run, the risk of permanent damage to the exhaust system makes removal of the 'cat' a sensible proposition if there is any doubt regarding the availability of unleaded petrol during your tour.

Carburettor engines

Engines with carburettors generally have a much simpler fuel-delivery system, mechanically and atmospherically controlled, and as such they tend to be adjusted to function efficiently over as wide a range of conditions as possible. They are still susceptible to variations in octane rating but as they are not, as a rule, controlled by an engine control unit (ECU) there is no way of adjusting the air/fuel mixture 'on the fly'. The carburettor's fuel/air ratio is fixed by the size of its various jets: the larger the jet's value the more fuel it will pass into the airflow, which enriches the mixture; conversely, smaller jets allow less fuel into the airflow, which will weaken the mixture.

As most carburettors are pre-set to function well within around 1,000m of sea level under most riding conditions, you will not experience any problems if you climb the occasional hill. However, venture significantly above this altitude and you will start to notice a definite reduction in power, and possibly also the way in which the engine responds to throttle input. At altitude our atmosphere is thinner, or at a lower pressure, so – remembering the relationship between airflow and fuel content – it also follows that altitude has an effect on the amount of fuel entering the engine, and therefore the power it produces. Consider that at sea level we experience air pressure of 1.0ATM (atmosphere), but that at an altitude of around 3,000m air pressure drops to 0.71ATM. That means there is 29% less air going into the engine, and therefore 29% less fuel too.

If you are embarking on a journey that entails a lot of riding

ignition/fuelling systems can produce high power outputs from a surprisingly small amount of the appropriate fuel. These developments have made demands on producers to improve various characteristics of the fuels they create. The most obvious difference for the motorist is seen in the fuel's octane rating, although the significance of this is rarely understood.

Without going into too many of the principles of thermodynamics, a fuel's octane rating is an indication of how much compression it can withstand before spontaneous ignition occurs. In simple terms, the more you squeeze or compress a gas (in this case the fuel/air mix that is drawn into the cylinder) the hotter it will get. A gaseous low-octane fuel/air mix can resist a compression ratio of, say, 8:1, but compress it further, say to 11:1, and the heat that this extra compression generates will be sufficient to cause it to self-ignite in certain conditions. As the efficient and controlled running of the engine depends on an accurate point of combustion determined by the spark at the plug, it is obvious that uncontrolled self-ignition is not at all desirable and could, in the long term, cause some fairly serious damage to the engine.

The noise an engine makes if the fuel/air mix burns too soon in its cycle is what we call 'knocking' or 'pinking', and will generally be heard as a 'tinkling' noise when the engine is under load. As the majority of modern engines rely upon higher cylinder compression for their increased power output, it is essential that the combination of fuel/air mixture and ignition timing remain in the optimum range. Thankfully, some modern engine management systems can be reprogrammed to accommodate this lower grade fuel by retarding the ignition timing; indeed, some ECUs are sophisticated enough to sense this pre-ignition and retard the timing automatically, but care should be taken and your dealer consulted for confirmation and ECU reprogramming if necessary.

at high altitude ('high altitude' is considered to be anything in excess of 8,000ft) it makes a lot of sense to look at being able to increase the carburettor jet sizes to enrich the air/fuel mixture, and restore some of the lost power. The downside of this, of course, is that you have to readjust the jetting once you return to lower altitudes, otherwise you run the risk of the engine running excessively rich.

Fuel-injected engines

Fuel injection was once thought of as a performance enhancement usually found on large prestige cars, but the old systems were generally very inefficient and wasteful of fuel. However, fuel injection has rapidly become the only way to meet the increasingly strict exhaust emission controls being imposed upon engine manufacturers. Modern systems rely upon a raft of technologies – complex computer control of fuel delivery and ignition timing combined with exhaust gas analysing (lambda) sensors and catalytic converters – to meet these environmental obligations. These systems are sophisticated enough to be self-calibrating, with the ECU constantly monitoring and adjusting the relationship between fuel delivered and exhaust gas temperature to ensure that a constant and consistent fuel/air ratio is achieved. Fuel injection systems can be flexible enough to allow the engine to cope with a reasonable range of fuel octanes, but the ECU may need reprogramming to be able to use the very low octane ratings found in some areas.

Cooling systems

All internal combustion engines produce heat as a by-product of their operation, and this heat somehow has to be dissipated to ensure that the engine remains within its optimum temperature range. Air-cooled engines such as the BMW boxer twin rely upon cooling fins cast into the cylinder and engine casings to increase their surface area, allowing maximum transferred heat loss. Liquid-cooled engines have a pressurised system with a front-mounted radiator very similar to the type found in cars. Both types of system rely entirely upon airflow to do their work, and without that cooling flow of air through the engine great damage can be caused.

Carburettor

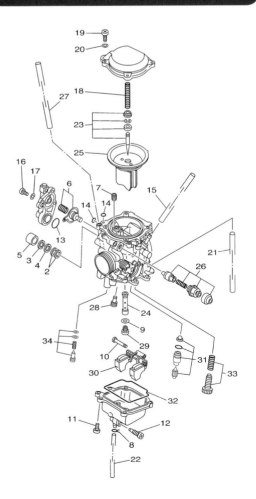

Fuel injection

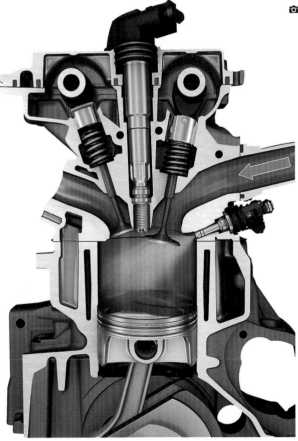

◣ **Modern fuel injection systems are ultra-efficient.**
📷 Author

Air-cooled engines

An air-cooled engine's cooling system has essentially only one moving part, and that is the air around it, but that air has to get to the engine and circulate around it to keep it cool. The cooling fins cast onto the cylinder or cylinders must be kept completely free from any obstruction or blockage such as mud or foliage that might prevent air flowing across the engine. Check that any supplementary cooling systems also remain clear – on some bikes you will find an oil cooler tucked up underneath the front fender. Cool oil does its job much better than hot, thin oil so it is imperative that the oil cooler is operating at maximum efficiency.

Liquid-cooled engines

Liquid-cooled systems offer some advantages over air cooling, although they need a constant airflow to operate effectively. Liquid coolant is pumped around the engine through a series of waterways, picking up heat as it goes. Flexible pipes then take the hot liquid to the radiator where it is cooled by airflow. The cooled liquid is circulated back to the hot engine where it goes through the cycle again.

Liquid-cooled systems are thermostatically controlled to ensure that they come up to operating temperature very quickly, and an additional electric fan is installed to create additional airflow if the engine gets too hot. In this way it can operate over a very wide range of temperatures while keeping the engine at a reasonably constant temperature.

Modern coolants also perform other functions within the engine itself, and have been formulated to prevent internal corrosion and deposits of scale or sludge within the system. A quality coolant must always be used, and diluted to the concentration level appropriate for the ambient operating temperatures.

Wheels, brakes and tyres

Any of the 'cycle parts' of a motorcycle must be considered critical components as they allow the motorcycle to move and are used by the rider to control every aspect of the bike's progress. Wheels do not need simply to rotate: the rear wheel has to transmit the engine's power to the ground to give drive and forward progress, the front needs to be able to transfer steering input, and both need to be able to deal with the enormous forces they will be subjected to under braking and cornering. Your bike will have one of two types of wheel – spoked or cast – which are two very different designs, both of which have their individual merits.

Cast wheels

Cast wheels are of single-piece construction, manufactured and machined from a specialist aluminium alloy. In use they tend to be a little stiffer than spoked wheels, and they are generally fitted with a tubeless tyre. Their aesthetic appeal and freedom from regular maintenance makes them more suited to road use. If they are used for serious off-road terrain, extreme care must be taken not to subject them to high stress loadings, which might cause a crack in the rim, seriously weakening the wheel and allowing tyre deflation.

Spoked wheels

Spoked wheels, on the other hand, have very many more components and consist of a rim which is generally a rolled and welded aluminium extrusion connected with high-tensile steel spokes to a separate wheel hub into which the bearings are mounted. This very different construction gives an extremely strong but resilient wheel which is capable of withstanding great stresses but can also flex a little when subjected to extreme load. It is this degree of flexibility and

Cast wheel

Spoked wheel

← Each type of wheel has its advantages.
📷 BMW Motorrad

multi-component construction that makes spoked wheels very suitable for the rigours of off-road use. If they suffer a heavy impact, from a boulder or a trench edge, for example, the radial pattern of the spokes will spread the shock-load over a greater area, reducing the risk of damage to the wheel. If the wheel rim or any of the spokes are damaged they can be replaced or the wheel rebuilt, although this is a specialist task.

Brakes

All adventure motorcycles are equipped with hydraulic brakes, and in a lot of cases these systems will be augmented by an anti-lock braking system (ABS). The performance range of an ABS system is pre-set by the manufacturer, and on certain models it cannot even be switched off. The hydraulics work on basic principles, though, with the effort applied to the brake lever being multiplied by the cylinder diameters and transferred via an incompressible fluid to the brake pads, which in turn act on the brake disc. These systems rely upon the incompressibility of the brake fluid to work, but the brake fluid will degrade over time so it needs to be changed regularly. And one of its biggest weaknesses is that it is hygroscopic – an avid absorber of water.

Failing brake performance is an obvious sign that something in this critical system is wrong and needs attention. If the brakes start making odd noises, like excessive squealing or grinding under braking, then the pads are probably worn and need replacing. If the lever travel is always excessive or feels 'spongy' then you probably have air bubbles in the system. These will need to be removed by bleeding the brakes, or purging any trapped air from the brake lines and calipers (see pages 98–100).

If your brakes work well initially but subsequently suffer

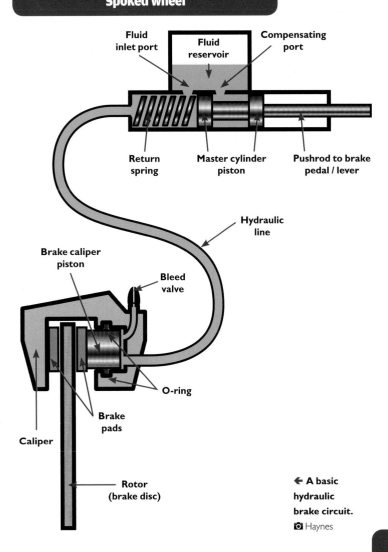

← A basic hydraulic brake circuit.
📷 Haynes

Tyres and tubes

From simple beginnings, the technology involved in modern tyre development has advanced tremendously in recent years. Tyre profile, carcass construction, tread pattern and compound, tubed or tubeless – these are all factors that should be taken into consideration when you think about tyres. As the only thing separating you from painful contact with the road is a half-inch thickness of rubber, making a visual inspection of your tyres before every ride is a good habit to get into that does not take much time. Having the correct air pressure in the tyres is also critical and should never be taken for granted.

Over-inflated tyres will wear unevenly and give a very harsh ride as well as compromising grip levels. When looking at your tyres, check for any unusual tread-wear patterns which might indicate a problem. If one side of your tyre is showing more wear than the other your wheels may be misaligned, or at worst your chassis may have been damaged. Intermediate tyres with larger tread blocks can also suffer from tearing if they are subjected to hard off-road use, while extended periods of high-speed tarmac riding can make them become very hot indeed, especially if they are slightly soft. As tyre rubber warms up it also gets softer and this decreases its resilience, so always check for any cracks or tearing between the tread block and the tyre after a long run.

An under-inflated tyre will also wear unevenly, but critically the increased flexion it sustains will greatly increase

from excessive lever travel under heavy braking, then the brake fluid is most probably contaminated with moisture. As was mentioned earlier in this section, brake fluid is hygroscopic, but its boiling point, at 230°C, is far higher than that of water. If the brake fluid gets hotter than 100°C, any absorbed water it contains will vaporise, releasing microscopic bubbles of water vapour. These bubbles are highly compressible and can cause a more-or-less instant – and catastrophic – reduction in braking ability exactly when you need it most!

Cheaper or low-performance brake pads tend to lose their effectiveness when they get too hot. If your brakes fade under heavy braking then you probably have the wrong grade of brake pad in the calipers and will need to fit more suitable items.

its running temperature, and if it gets hot enough the tyre casing or inner tube may start to degrade, a process that will end up in a catastrophic failure. Don't forget that carrying extra weight, such as luggage or a passenger, or travelling at high speeds for long periods of time will also increase the load on your tyres and they will require extra pressure. Check your manual for the recommended figures and keep your pressure gauge handy!

Suffering a puncture need not be the end of the world, or indeed the end of the tyre. Most punctures in a tubeless tyre, certainly up to 5mm, can be repaired as long as they are within the central area of the treaded surface of the tyre. Emergency kits are available that will plug the hole temporarily, but a proper repair must be made as soon as practicable. Tyres damaged outside that area or on the sidewall will require replacement.

Tubed tyres

The nature of tyres with inner tubes means that they can take a little more punishment than their tubeless cousins as they are not as reliant on the total integrity of the tyre casing to keep them inflated. Once the puncturing object has been removed, the inner tube can be simply repaired with a vulcanised patch, and as long as the tyre has not suffered major damage it can be refitted.

Puncture prevention products

Care should be taken if you elect to use one of the many puncture prevention products available today. These are usually a liquid polymer compound, sometimes reinforced with small fibres, which remains semi-liquid within the tyre or tube, working on the principle that the air pressure in the tyre will force the solution into the puncture, creating a self-sealing plug. This should only ever be looked on as a temporary fix and the puncture should be repaired as soon as possible. Also, these solutions can very often cause problems with repairing tubeless tyres as they leave a sticky residue over the entire inner surface of the tyre that can be troublesome to remove. With a tubed tyre, if the puncturing object is left in place, it can potentially cause far more damage by lacerating or tearing the inner tube, making it impossible to repair.

Transmission systems
Shaft drive

Shaft-drive systems are often thought of as being maintenance-free, but this is far from the truth! The mechanisms comprising a modern shaft drive are very complex, and while they do not need daily care, they still need to be maintained according to the manufacturer's schedule. As the shaft drive has evolved, it has developed from a fairly crude bevel drive into a sophisticated and highly efficient gearbox. The design of the gears and the tolerances to which they are manufactured make them

← A lucky escape!
📷 Krzysztof Samborski

← Even tyre sealant has its limits!
📷 Gary Burns

⬇ Puncture repairs are easy when you know how.
📷 Author

↑ **Shaft drive systems can be heavy and bulky.**
📷 BMW Motorrad

↑ **Drive chains need to be kept clean and lubricated.**
📷 Thorvaldur Orn Kristmundsson

smooth and quiet in operation. To achieve this degree of efficiency, however, they need high levels of lubrication and must be aligned to a high degree of accuracy. Rubber boots or gaiters need to be in tip-top condition to prevent ingress of dust or dirt, and shaft splines need to be kept lubricated with a molybdenum-based grease. Hub oil seals need to be checked and if necessary replaced on a periodic basis to avoid failure, and of course the oil level must be checked and oil replaced in accordance with the manufacturer's schedule.

Chain drive

With the growth in popularity of large, shaft-driven adventure bikes the humble articulated roller link transmission chain might be thought to be redundant.

⬇ **Roller transmission chains are remarkably efficient.**
📷 Author

Chain drive, however, is still in regular use by the majority of more off-road-oriented machinery – all KTM models, BMW's F800GS and the 'X' series, and the new Triumph Tiger XC are good examples. Drive chains are an extremely flexible and relatively efficient option in terms of energy transmission and, if properly looked after, will last quite a long time, sometimes in excess of 30,000 miles.

Correct adjustment and regular lubrication is also critical with chain drives, both in terms of energy efficiency and component life. A badly adjusted or misaligned chain can affect many aspects of the bike. If it is loose it can wear the drive sprockets in a remarkably short length of time; even worse, if left too loose, it could jump the sprockets altogether, causing a great deal of damage to the engine casings. If the tension is too great then the output shaft bearing can suffer, and there is a greater risk of snapping a chain if the suspension is fully compressed.

A roller transmission chain might look quite simple, but the reality is that it is made from hundreds of small yet precisely machined parts, all of which must fit with each other and be compatible with the gear wheels or sprockets. As with any moving component with metal-to-metal contact, lubrication is key to the reduction of friction (and therefore power losses) and undue wear. The total bearing surface of a roller chain is surprisingly large, and if you consider the forces applied to it and the harshness of the environment in which it has to function, it is no surprise that it needs regular maintenance.

Electrical systems

A bike's electrical system is a very complex network, with interconnected cables and switches determining where and when power is delivered to various components and accessories. Some of these items are manually controlled by the rider while others are controlled by the machine itself, but the purpose of any electrical circuit is to deliver electrical power. Interrupt that network or break a connection and power will be lost – not necessarily entirely, as some parts of the network are independent – but a broken wire somewhere in your wiring harness means that *something* will not function as expected or required.

Electrical power is fundamental to the motorcycle, but it has to be generated, stored and distributed for it to work for the bike. An alternator generates the electricity and is driven by the bike's engine. It can be mounted inside the engine casings, generally on one end of the crankshaft, or it can be mounted externally – piggybacked – with a separate chain drive. The electrical energy it produces is stored in the bike's battery ready for it to be used by any component that needs it. The charging current delivered from the alternator to the battery is controlled by a voltage regulator/rectifier which converts the alternator's AC

(alternating current) output to DC (direct current) which will charge the battery, and regulates its output within the range of 13.5 to 14.5 volts. When working normally the regulator will sense when the battery is full and will dissipate surplus energy in the form of heat.

Power from the battery is not an endless supply, however, and care must be taken not to use more than the alternator can generate. If this happens for a brief period the battery will be able to make up the shortfall by providing the additional power needed, but using a lot of accessories for an extended period can quite quickly deplete the battery's power reserve, and that may leave you stranded and unable to start the machine.

The switchgear on your bike might look simple from the outside but it has to distribute power to a large number of components. A simple turn of the ignition switch might complete two or three separate circuits, for example, and the wiring loom attached to it might be built of up to eight separate wires, depending on what is being switched.

⬇ Colour coding makes it easier to identify current tracks. Even a fairly basic bike can have a complicated wiring loom – this diagram is for a 1994–96 BMW F650.
📷 Haynes

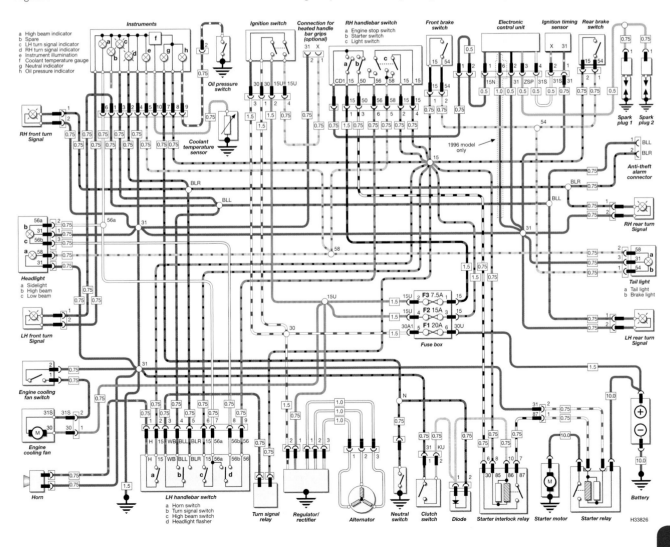

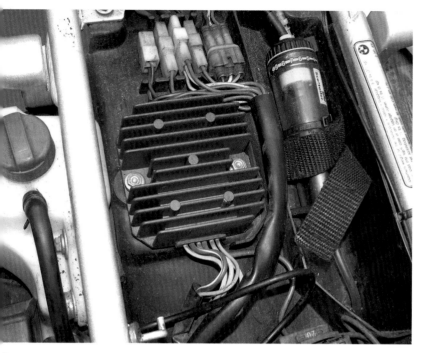

Batteries

Motorcycle battery technology is constantly advancing, and developments have created a battery which is very different from the liquid-filled lead/acid batteries that were virtually ubiquitous a decade ago. A typical modern battery will be fully sealed and described as 'maintenance-free' (MF), with an electrolytic gel used in place of the liquid acid found in older batteries. This type of battery is ideal for use in motorcycles as it tends to be smaller, far more robust and unaffected by position or orientation. It will operate under a wide range of conditions, and deliver high current rates when required.

A motorcycle battery has only two real enemies – overcharging and deep discharging – and both can do some serious damage. Charging any battery creates gases (hydrogen and oxygen) as part of the electrolytic process. These gases build up in proportion to the charging voltage, and unless vented can cause the battery casing to deform. Charging the battery also generates a certain amount of heat, which is quite normal. If there is a problem with the battery, however, or if the battery is already fully charged, this heat can build up and cause deformation of the casing and the internal plates. If the battery is left overcharging the heat created can cause the electrolyte to evaporate, further concentrating the sulphuric acid. If caught in time, this can be resolved by disconnecting the charger and replenishing the electrolyte with distilled or de-ionised water to restore the correct electrolytic balance. If left overcharging, though, the build-up of heat can either boil the battery dry or buckle the plates, with the consequential risk of causing an internal

↑ There is not much cooling airflow under the seat for a typical voltage-regulating relay (VRR).
📷 Haynes

Under the skin, the switches themselves are very complex components and need to work smoothly and effectively to deliver the power where it needs to go. A dry film aerosol lubricant such as WD40 will penetrate the smallest parts of the switchgear, cleaning and lubricating as it goes, keeping the switches moving freely and keeping corrosion at bay.

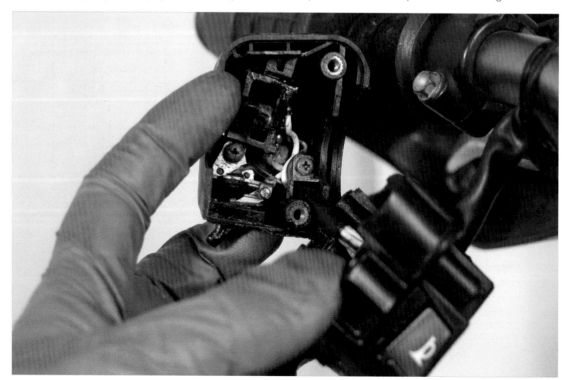

➜ Older mechanical switches can suffer from dirt and corrosion.
📷 Author

← The internal
view of a typical
lead/acid battery.
📷 Yuasa UK Ltd.

short circuit. As the combination of hydrogen and oxygen produced by charging is highly flammable, there is a very real risk of an explosion which could shatter the battery casing, spraying the extremely acidic electrolyte everywhere – not a very desirable outcome!

This risk of overcharging can be reduced by the use of an 'intelligent' charger, which is especially useful if the bike is to be stored for long periods. Also known as a battery optimiser, this is a high-tech battery charging solution which constantly monitors the condition of the battery and delivers just enough charge to keep it at its optimum charge level. As the charging voltage never exceeds what is required, there is little chance of the battery failing as a result of anything other than reaching the end of its natural life.

Deep discharges, on the other hand, can do as much, if not more, long-term damage to a battery. In normal usage, a battery will produce – as a by-product of the electrolytic process – lead sulphate formed as soft crystals between the plates. During the battery's recharging cycle, these soft crystals are redissolved, restoring the chemical properties of the electrolyte. Care must be exercised when charging a sealed or maintenance-free (MF) battery, as their design requires them to be charged at a lower rate to prevent excessive gassing, which requires the use of a specific charger.

If a lead/acid charger is used for an MF battery there is a good chance that the battery will overcharge, causing the gel electrolyte to break down and produce gases. As the MF battery's casing is sealed, these gases will build up pressure and distort the casing, leading to failure.

If the battery is left in a discharged state, however, or has a small but permanent load like a clock or an alarm, over time these soft lead sulphate crystals will transform into hard lead sulphate, and can consolidate into larger physical particles which will continue to crystallise and grow. The presence of these crystals in the battery initially creates a small decrease in the battery's capacity and this can 'fool' a charging system into overcharging the battery, with the previously discussed consequences. If left in low-charge condition, these crystals can grow large enough to occupy all the space between the plates of a battery, causing them to buckle and eventually short out, killing the battery. A sulphated battery may show an initial response to charging, but its revival is always short-lived and it will inevitably fail.

A battery specialist will have the necessary test equipment to fully evaluate a battery's condition, but with a multi-meter you can perform a couple of basic tests which will give you a good idea of the battery's condition.

Servicing

Andreas Hülsmann

Many of us will have previously left the maintenance of our motorcycle to a dealer or a garage – they are the experts. But what happens when you are out on the trail, far from a garage or a dealer, and are confronted with a problem that you need to resolve? By having a good level of knowledge of your bike and its basic functions, you will be in a much better position to assess your situation and get yourself out of trouble. In this section we will take a look at just how simple some of these tasks are, and how easily they can be achieved with a modest selection of tools. Performing just a few simple maintenance tasks is the best way to get to know your motorcycle, and doing it in the comfort of your home environment first gives you the opportunity to learn and assimilate the skills that you might one day need to use on a trip.

There is no 'dark art' to looking after your bike. While specific procedures might vary between different bikes, most of the fundamentals are all pretty similar. Your bike will have been delivered with an owner's handbook of some kind, but this will only cover the most basic elements of maintenance. In this part of the book we will take a closer look at a variety of tasks and the basic principles behind them.

The previous chapter gave an overview of the fundamental principles behind a modern motorcycle and how it works, and here we will look at the implementation of those principles, and how they are relevant to the bike you own. Bear in mind, however, that there is no substitute for having a detailed workshop manual, which gives a greater level of specific detail relevant to your particular motorcycle. Haynes, of course, offers a comprehensive range of titles covering almost every popular motorcycle!

Engine servicing

You can often start to feel when the oil needs changing
in the bike, because gear changes might not be quite so
slick and engine noise might increase. It is at this point that
the lubricant will need changing. Oil will flow more readily
when it is warm, so before doing the oil change either
start the bike and let it idle for a few minutes, or take it

DISPOSAL OF ENGINE OIL

**Used engine oil is nasty stuff, dangerous
to both personal health and the
environment. Disposal facilities exist at most
if not all recycling sites, and old oil quite
simply must be disposed of in a morally and
socially acceptable way. If you are travelling in
third world countries, you might find that your
'old' oil will be perfect for a local's ancient
Peugeot, so see if it can be recycled that way.**

for a short ride. The only tools required are spanners, an
oil filter wrench or cartridge tool, and a drain tray.

Remove any obstructions like bash-plates or engine bars
which might interfere with the operation, and identify the
oil drain plug – it could be in the centre of the sump, or
offset to one side. Support the bike upright or on the side
stand, depending on the position of the drain plug. Place
the drain tray under the bike ready to catch the old oil, then
loosen and carefully remove the drain plug. If your plug is
magnetised, use a rag to remove any particles that might be
stuck to it. When all the oil has drained, refit the drain plug
using a fresh sealing washer and tighten to the torque figure
quoted in your manual.

The oil filter cartridge can be safely and easily removed
with a special tool. Once it has been removed, drain any oil it
contains back into the drip tray. Lubricate the rubber oil seal
of the new filter with a small amount of clean engine oil and
re-install the new cartridge. Cartridge oil filters are mostly
designed to be installed and tightened by hand. Do not use
a strap wrench or a chain tool to tighten as this can damage
the internal structure of the filter, and make it very difficult
to remove for the next change.

Refill with the specified amount and type of clean oil and check the level with the dipstick or sight glass. Avoid using oils designed for car engines which contain friction modifiers and will cause wet clutch systems to slip. Run the engine for a few minutes at a fast idle to circulate and warm the oil, turn the engine off and let it stand for a minute or two. Check the level again, and adjust as necessary.

Brake checks

Without doubt, the most critical safety system on the bike is braking, and it is imperative that the brakes are in the best condition at all times. If you notice any deficiency or deterioration in performance, or the brakes start to make strange noises, then the time has come to have a good look to see what is going wrong. Getting the best out of your brakes is quite simple, and spending a little time and effort performing some simple visual checks will flag up any potential problems before they become serious or dangerous.

Checking brake pad material

Use the centre stand or some other means of support to hold either of the wheels off the ground. Spin the wheel and listen for any signs of the brake binding. Take a look into the caliper to assess how much friction material remains on the pad. Worn brake pads can seriously compromise brake performance, and may cause irreparable damage to the brake disc if they are allowed to wear too far. Most brake pads have a minimum wear indicator, usually a groove cut into the friction material – if the pads have been worn down so much that the groove is no longer visible it is time to replace them.

Checking brake lines

Inspect the brake hoses from top to bottom, paying particular attention to any area where they could chafe against the bodywork or chassis parts. If any older style of rubber-sheathed hose shows signs of cracking it will need replacing. Resolve the cause of any rubbing or chafing, which will cause longer-term damage to the hose.

Checking brake fluid

The quantity and condition of your brake fluid is paramount to the effective performance of your brakes. As the brake material wears down the fluid level in the reservoir falls accordingly, so if the fluid level falls too low there is a danger that air might be sucked into the system, which will render the brakes ineffective. The brake fluid can also degrade over time, usually indicated by a change in its colour. Fresh fluid will normally be clear and straw or honey-coloured; contaminated fluid is often a much darker colour and can sometimes be almost black and opaque. If you see this then the fluid must be changed as a matter of some urgency – see the section on page 98.

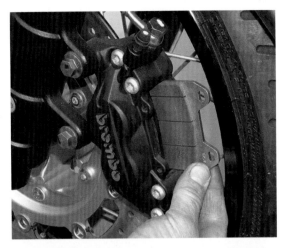

← Most caliper designs allow you to get a good look at the pads without having to remove them, but removal is a good opportunity to give everything a quick clean.
📷 Haynes

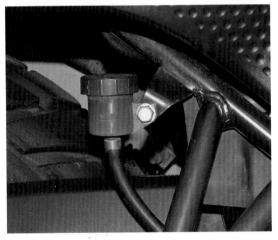

← When the fluid reservoir is dirty it is difficult to judge the condition of the fluid within.
📷 Haynes

The brake fluid reservoir will have minimum and maximum marks, so make sure that the fluid level remains within these limits at all times. Before topping up your reservoir, check that you have a fresh bottle of the correct grade of brake fluid. This will generally be DOT4, but check the reservoir cap as this will usually show the type required. Make sure the bike is upright and that the reservoir is horizontal, then unscrew the reservoir cap (some models may have a tamper-proof cap, so check in your manual before attempting to remove it) and remove the bellows seal underneath. Pour fresh fluid carefully into the reservoir, to a level between the minimum and maximum lines. Put the bellows seal back on, followed by the reservoir cap. Brake fluid is a very effective paint-stripper, so take care at every stage of this operation not to spill or splash brake fluid on to your bike's bodywork. When you have completed this operation, pump the brake lever to reset the pads against the disc and verify the brake action. The procedure is the same for the rear brake, but extra care must be taken when working on the rear brake as the master cylinder reservoir is usually much smaller than the front and will contain much less brake fluid.

BMW R1200GS
SERVICING

Without any doubt, the BMW GS boxer twin is the forefather of adventure motorcycles. The legend was born in the late 1970s as a prototyped R80, and BMW gave it the family suffix of G/S (short for *Gelände/Strasse*, which translates as trail/road). Never before had such an appropriate name been given to a motorcycle, or indeed had a new genre of motorcycling been created by one model.

At its official launch in 1980, the R80G/S represented a huge step forward in the development of motorcycling. Not only was it the lightest 800cc motorcycle, it was also the fastest trail bike in the world at the time – and it had the quickest rear wheel change! Its growth in popularity can only be described as meteoric, as it took 20% of all BMW motorcycle sales in the year following its launch.

Subsequent years saw technical developments and innovations introduced throughout the range, with the monolever single-sided swing-arm combined with a shaft drive being a constant feature of the bike until the mid-1980s. Of these early models the R80G/S-PD 'Paris–Dakar' variant is still thought to be an iconic motorcycle, with styling derived from BMW's Paris–Dakar race winners.

In 1987 came the start of the evolution of the motorcycles into the range we recognise today. The older monolever was replaced with BMW's Paralever system for reduced 'shaft effect' and greater strength of the swing-arm. The range was augmented by the larger 980cc R100 engine, and the family renamed the GS – meaning *Gelände/Sport*. This revised range carried on with various developments of the 60hp boxer twin used in most models through to the 1994 R100GS Paris–Dakar.

With a wheels-up redesign in 1994, the new GS range saw the introduction of the revolutionary tele-lever front-fork system, which produced hitherto unknown levels of handling and response in a road motorcycle. The unburstable engine was given four-valve heads and an increase in power from 60 to 80hp, while rock-solid handling combined with off-road ability made the 1994 R1100GS instantly recognisable as an overlanding motorcycle.

The journey of the GS to the present day included technological innovation with almost every model year, super-efficient engine management systems and a CAN-bus electrical control system. The ADV variant of the bikes received massive 30-litre fuel tanks, improved weather protection as well as 'enduro' gearing for better all-terrain performance, and programmable ignition to allow the use of low-octane fuel. The introduction of servo-assisted brakes was a 'first' in 2002, although they no longer feature in the current GS range.

The current R1200GS retains all the characteristics of its heritage and provides day-long riding comfort over all terrains, while technological advances have allowed the original 'boxer' twin engine to produce over 110hp with an impressive 85ft/lb of torque. It is truly a legend among modern motorcycles.

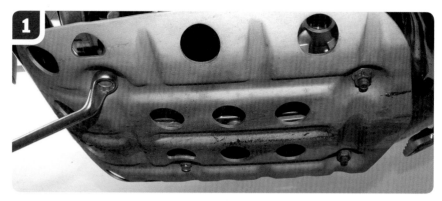

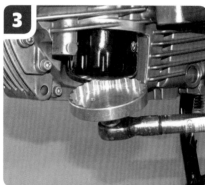

arming the engine will help the oil drain easily. Support the bike on its centre stand and ensure it is stable and on level ground.

1. Remove and withdraw the sump guard.
2. Unscrew the oil drain plug and allow the old oil to drain into the drain pan.
3. Remove the old oil filter using an appropriate tool, catching any residual oil in the drain pan.
4. Clean the area around the filter mounting point and install the new filter, remembering to lubricate the filter seal ring.
5. Using an appropriate wrench, tighten the filter to the specified torque figure.
6. Refit the drain plug using a new sealing washer if available, and tighten to the specified torque setting. Refill the engine with the correct amount and grade of oil.
7. Check the oil level in the inspection window before refitting the filler cap, using a new seal if necessary. Start the engine and allow it to idle for a few minutes to distribute the oil. Stop the engine and recheck the oil level window after a few minutes, adding more oil if required to reach the correct level.

A clogged air filter will make your engine run badly and will ruin your fuel consumption. Thankfully it is an easy component to replace.

1 Remove the rider's seat and right-hand tank covers to gain access to the filter housing.
2 Pull out the locating clips which secure the filter housing.
3 Prise the duct off, noting the position of the mounting lug on its rear face.
4 Remove the old filter – inspect and clean or replace as necessary.
5 Install the new filter, taking care not to damage the element. Ensure it is correctly seated.
6 Replace the air duct, ensuring the correct location of the mounting lug, and secure the clips.
7 Refit the tank cover and panel, followed by the rider's seat.

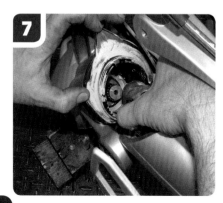

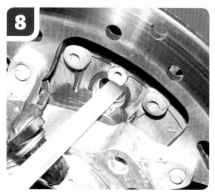

Support the bike on its centre stand and ensure it is stable and on level ground.

1 Remove the rear wheel and splashguard. Support the final drive unit with an axle stand or block of wood.

2 Displace the rear brake caliper and secure it to the rear subframe. Do not allow it to hang on the brake pipe!

3 Remove the rear-wheel speed sensor, and release sufficient cable to secure it alongside the brake caliper on the rear subframe. Take care not to lose the 'O' ring seal. Cut and remove the cable tie securing the driveshaft housing boot to the driveshaft housing.

4 Loosen the oil level bolt, leaving it in place.

5 Loosen the rear Paralever mounting bolt.

6 Support the drive housing as you withdraw the rear Paralever mounting bolt, then carefully tilt the housing back until the oil level bolt is at the 6 o'clock position. Note that the driveshaft coupling will disengage from the final drive as the housing is lowered.

7 Remove the oil level bolt fully, and allow the oil to drain into the drain pan. When the oil has drained completely, lift the final drive unit and re-engage the splined end of the bevel gear inside the driveshaft coupling. Secure the Paralever arm to the housing with its bolt and tighten to the specified torque figure, using a thread-locking compound.

8 Refit the driveshaft housing boot, securing it with a new cable tie. Refill the final drive unit with the correct volume of the specified oil. It can be filled via the speed sensor mounting hole or the oil level plug hole. Refit the oil level plug and the speed sensor using new sealing washers or 'O' rings where required. Install the remaining components in the reverse order of removal.

Final drive oil service (07-on models)

Support the bike on its centre stand and ensure it is stable and on level ground.

1 Loosen and remove the final drive oil drain plug on the rear of the housing. Use a piece of cardboard or similar to direct the oil into the drain pan. When the old oil has completely drained refit the plug and tighten to the specified torque.

2 Remove the final drive housing oil filler plug, removing the rear wheel if better access is required. Refill the final drive housing with the correct amount of the specified oil, refit the filler plug and tighten it to the specified torque.

Gearbox oil service

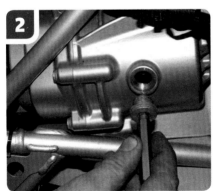

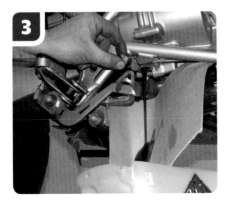

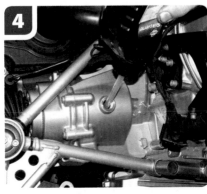

The BMW is unusual in having separate lubrication systems for the engine and gearbox. As a rule of thumb, the gearbox oil must be replaced every fourth major oil change (24,000 miles).

1 Support the bike on its centre stand and ensure it is stable and on level ground.
2 Remove the gearbox oil filler plug.
3 Loosen and remove the gearbox oil drain plug, using a piece of cardboard or similar to direct the oil into the drain pan.
4 Refit the gearbox oil drain plug using a new sealing washer and tighten it to the specified torque setting. Refill the gearbox with the specified oil to the lower edge of the filler hole, and refit the gearbox oil filler plug using a new sealing washer. Tighten to the specified torque setting.

Ensure the bike is secure and stable, preferably on its centre stand.

1 Remove the 'R' clip from the pad pin.
2 Unscrew the pad pin from the caliper.
3 Remove the pad spring.
4 Remove the old pads from the caliper.
5 Push the pistons back into the caliper using hand pressure only. Smear a small amount of copper-based brake grease on the pads before installation, ensuring correct orientation in the caliper.
6 Refit the pad spring.
7 Clean and lubricate the pad pin with a little brake grease before reinstalling it in the caliper. Be sure that it passes through both pads and tighten it to the specified torque setting (some models use a push-fit pad pin as shown).
8 Refit the 'R' clip to secure the pad pin and actuate the brake lever several times to re-seat the pads on the discs.

Ensure the bike is secure and stable, preferably on its centre stand.

1 After removing the spray guard, remove the 'R' clip from the pad pin.
2 Use a suitable punch to drive out the pad pin.
3 Withdraw the pads from the rear of the caliper.
4 Check the condition of the pads, replacing them if worn. If they are within wear limits they can be cleaned using an oil-free fine wire brush and a solvent-based brake cleaner.
5 Gently push the pistons back into the caliper before installing the brake pads. A little brake grease smeared on the backs of the pads will help prevent brake squeal. Ensure the pads are correctly oriented in the caliper before reinstalling the cleaned and lubricated pad pin.
6 Secure the pad pin with the 'R' clip before actuating the brake pedal several times to re-set the pads against the disc surface. Refit the spray guard.

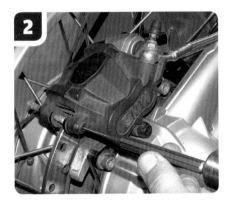

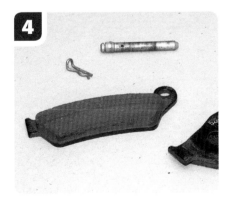

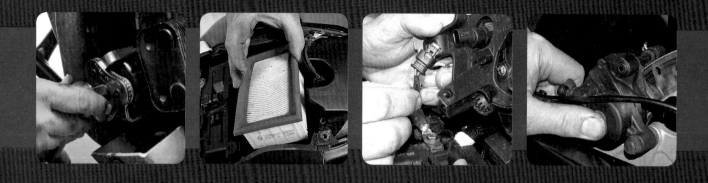

BMW F800GS/F650GS (TWIN)
SERVICING

With the introduction of the 'F' series twins in 2008, BMW started to break the boxer twin's exclusive hold on the adventure motorcycle sector. Using skills and technology learned from the constant development of their smaller 'X' series bikes, the adoption of the Rotax parallel twin for the smaller bikes was a significant departure from their traditional 'boxer' or flat-twin layout. The use of this engine allowed for the design of a tall and slim bike, with all the advantages of having less weight and more agility for outstanding off-road performance.

There are two bikes in this branch of the family, the F800GS and its sibling the F650GS. Confusingly, both bikes have the same displacement of 798cc, but they are two very different motorcycles. The F650GS has a detuned version (70hp) of the same Rotax engine, as well as a lower seat height, simpler suspension and cast 19/17-inch wheel set. The F800GS has a greater power output of 85hp (65kW) and 59ft/lb (80Nm) of torque delivered at 5,750rpm, giving very punchy mid-range performance, ideally suited to off-roading.

Innovative engine management and fuelling systems have given both bikes impressive performance capabilities, both in terms of outright power and also in maximum fuel economy, with 200 miles (320km) easily achievable from a full 17-litre tank.

The suspension components fitted to the F800GS are relatively simple but complement the bike perfectly, giving over 8.5in (215mm) of travel, making off-road performance more than adequate for a bike of this size. The spoked wheels and tyres used in the optimal 21/17-inch combination give the bike impeccable road manners, and it is also available with a low-seat option, making it accessible to a greater range of riders. Complete the package with the additional options of ABS, heated grips and a fully functioning OBC and you have a bike which is more than a worthy competitor in the ADV arena.

Engine oil service

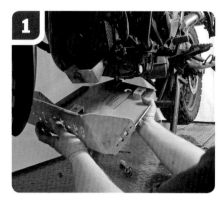

This operation should be performed with a warm engine – start the bike and allow it to idle until the cooling fan operates. Switch off and leave the bike for five minutes to allow the oil to return to the sump.

1. An aftermarket sump guard may need to be displaced. If you are changing the filter, some models require only the front mounting bolts to be removed, allowing the guard to pivot on its rear rubber-mounted bolts.

2. Place a drain tray underneath the sump and carefully remove the drain plug – remember the oil will be hot – and allow the sump to empty completely.

3. Refit the drain plug using a new sealing washer and tighten to the recommended torque figure.

4. If the oil filter requires replacement, remove it using a proprietary tool and catch any residual oil in the drain tray.

5. Clean the area around the mounting point, then lightly lubricate the new filter's sealing ring before installing the filter and tightening it to the specified torque figure. Do not use a strap wrench as this may damage the internal structure of the cartridge. If you do not have access to a torque wrench, then tightening as much as possible by hand will generally be adequate.

6. Replace the sump guard and refill the engine with the specified amount and type of fresh oil.

7. Start the engine and allow it to idle for a few minutes to circulate the oil. Stop the engine and let it to stand for five minutes before making the final oil level check, topping up as required to give the correct reading on the dipstick.

8. Replace and securely tighten the oil filler cap.

The F800GS keeps its air filter high and out of the way underneath the 'tank' cover. This makes changing it a genuine five-minute job, so now there is no excuse not to!

1 Remove the top 'tank' cover screws, four in the top cover and one on each side of the headstock. Unclip the power supply cables to the auxiliary power socket and remove the cover.

2 Undo the screws securing the filter cover and remove the cover.

3 Lift out the filter.

4 Inspect and clean the air filter – replace if necessary. If required, clean the inside of the air box with a lightly oiled cloth.

5 Install the new filter.

6 Refit the filter cover, ensuring the filter element is properly seated.

7 Reconnect the auxiliary power socket cable.

8 Refit the 'faux' tank cover.

Note: Manufacturers usually recommend that a paper-element filter should be replaced rather than cleaned. However, prolonged riding in dusty conditions will result in a paper filter becoming clogged very quickly, sometimes after just one day. In these circumstances it is acceptable to knock the dust out of the filter and carefully blow it clean from the reverse side. Replace the filter as soon as possible when returning to 'normal' riding conditions.

Front brake service

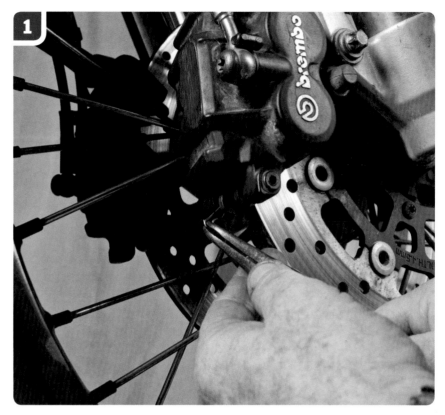

The brake systems on the F800GS are high-performance Brembo units designed for off-road use. All of the critical components are readily accessible, making replacement of any worn parts quick and easy.

1　If possible use hand pressure only to push the pistons back into the calipers. Withdraw the 'R' clip.
2　Push out the pad-retaining pin.
3　Withdraw the pads and discard if worn beyond service limits.
4　Clean and lubricate the pad-retaining pin, but replace if visibly worn.
5　Install new pads and locate with the pad-retaining pin. A smear of copper grease on the back of the pad will help prevent brake squeal.
6　Fully install the pad pin.
7　Install the 'R' clip to secure the pin in place. Pump the brake lever several times to seat the pads on the disc.

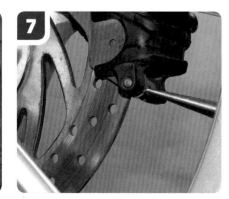

The front and rear brake calipers used on the F800GS are very similar in design and the same techniques can be employed. Always use braking components from approved manufacturers.

1 Push the caliper against the disc to force the piston back into the caliper to allow for the extra thickness of the new pads.
2 Withdraw the 'R' clip and push out the pad-retaining pin.
3 Withdraw the pads and discard if worn beyond service limits.
4 Clean and lubricate the pad-retaining pin, but replace if visibly worn.
5 Fit the innermost pad first and insert the pad pin part way to hold it in place. A smear of copper grease on the back of the pad will help prevent brake squeal.
6 Fully install the pad pin.
7 Install the 'R' clip to secure the pin in place. Pump the brake lever several times to seat the pads on the disc.

BMW F650GS/G650GS
SERVICING

Since its introduction to the market in 2000, the BMW F650GS (single) has always been one of the more understated performers in the ADV bike sector, and has largely been overshadowed by its big brother, the R1200GS. That said, it has always been an extremely competent motorcycle and is quietly efficient at almost everything it does. BMW's big single has always offered much more to the 'enduro' concept than just cosmetic styling. Rider ergonomics have been designed around the compromise of civilised road manners and off-road capability, and this combination has given the bike a multi-role versatility quite unlike any bike before it.

From the outset the F650GS was designed with overlanding in mind. The riding position is relaxed, but puts the rider firmly in control. Weight distribution is optimised with the adoption of an underseat fuel tank, which also helps keep the bike's centre of gravity low and greatly improves off-road stability and handling. The Rotax engine delivers high torque (63Nm), reliable power (50Hp) and models from 2005 onwards were redesigned with a twin-plug head

and given the latest BMS-CII engine control unit (ECU), which continually monitors and manages both fuelling and ignition curves according to the prevailing riding conditions. This later engine also uses a more advanced fuel injection system and a low-friction Nikasil-coated cylinder barrel to make it super-efficient, allowing the rider to comfortably achieve a range of over 200 miles from the 4.5-gallon tank. Uprated long-travel suspension and the torque of the big single-cylinder engine make it a perfect machine for overlanding, while the strength of its chassis means that it has the capacity to carry sufficient luggage for extended periods of time on the road.

The F650GS was discontinued in 2008 with the arrival of the parallel-twin models, but made a welcome return in 2009 in the form of an all-new model, known as the G650GS. In true BMW style the development did not stop there. In 2010 came the release of the G650GS 'Sertao', which with its wide handlebars, long-travel suspension and highly efficient 652cc single-cylinder engine is a worthy holder of the GS badge.

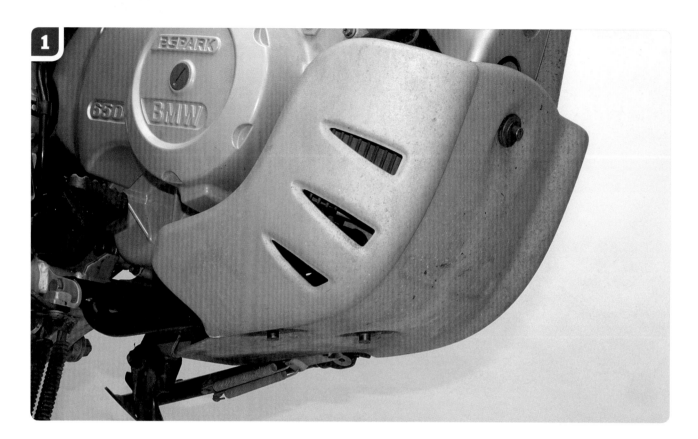

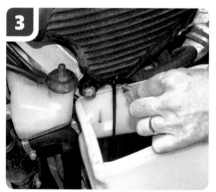

Ensure the bike is secure and standing on level ground. Warm the engine by running it at idle until the cooling fan comes on. Switch off, and let it stand for a few minutes to allow the oil to drain back into the sump.

1   Remove the sump guard and any other engine protection, the left-hand front side cover, and the engine sprocket cover.
2   Unscrew the oil filler cap to help the oil drain quickly, then put a clean drain pan underneath the oil tank on the left-hand side of the bike.
3   Unscrew the oil drain plug and allow the oil to drain from the tank.
4   Undo the screw at top-right corner of the tank and release the two clips bottom left.
5   Displace and tilt the tank to drain the residual oil. Refit the oil tank. Fit the drain plug using a new sealing washer and tighten it to the specified torque figure.
6   Support the bike vertically on the centre stand or an auxiliary stand. Place a clean drain tray beneath the engine and unscrew the sump drain plug.

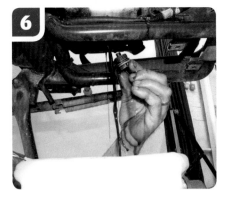

7 When the oil has completely drained, refit the drain plug using a new washer, and tighten it to the specified torque figure.

8 Working on the right-hand side of the bike, place a drain tray underneath the engine below the oil filter. Fabricate a chute cut from a plastic bottle, or use the approved BMW tool to direct the oil into the drain pan. Remove the filter cover.

9 Withdraw the old filter element.

10 Fit the new filter and refit the filter cover using a new seal if required.

11 Fill the oil tank with 2 litres of the specified oil, then start the engine and let it run at idle for 30 seconds. Turn the engine off and add another 0.3 litres of oil. Replace the filler cap and run the engine until it comes up to operating temperature.

12 Allow the engine to stand for a minute or two before making a final level check with the dipstick.

13 Replace the sprocket cover, side cover and sump protection, ensuring all fasteners are properly tightened and secure.

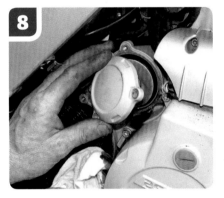

The F650GS houses its air box underneath a false 'tank' cover in the same way as the F800GS, but as the filter housing is mounted on the side of the air box slightly more work is required to remove the extra body panels.

1 Unscrew the various fasteners and remove the right-hand front side cover, noting the position of the panel peg and chassis grommet.
2 Disconnect the air sensor connector.
3 Unscrew the screws and withdraw the flange.
4 Withdraw the air duct.
5 Remove the filter element.
6 Tap the filter on a hard surface to dislodge any loose dust, then blow it clean with compressed air. Be sure to blow debris out of the filter in the reverse direction to normal airflow. If the filter cannot be cleaned then it must be replaced with a new one.
7 Reassemble in the reverse order, ensuring that the duct mounting lugs are correctly located.
8 Replace the locking flange and reconnect the air sensor connector before refitting the side cover.

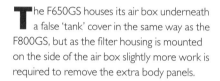

oth front and rear calipers on the F650GS are similar in design and the procedure described here (shown on a rear brake) can be equally applied.

1. Use hand pressure to push the caliper against the disc to ease the piston into the caliper. Remove the pad-retaining pin 'R' clip, noting its orientation and position.
2. Drive out the pad pin using a suitable punch or drift.
3. Remove the brake pads from the caliper. If they are within service limits, use a clean wire brush to restore their surfaces, otherwise replace them with a new set.
4. Fit the innermost pad first and insert the pad pin part way to hold it in place.
5. Fit the outermost pad and push the pin all the way through to the caliper.
6. Drive the pin fully home with a suitable punch or drift and refit the 'R' clip.
7. Actuate the brake lever several times to set the pads against the disc. Ensure correct braking operation before moving off.

KTM LC4 640 ADVENTURE
SERVICING

The KTM LC4 640 Adventure R is thought by many to be the perfect overlanding bike. Powered by KTM's evergreen LC4 motor, it has been the epitome of simplicity and function. First introduced as the '620' in 1997, the Adventure was a prominent feature of KTM's model range until it was discontinued in 2008 with the last model, the 640 Adventure, Travellers' Edition.

KTM never lost sight of their objective with the LC4 Adventure, and this is very apparent when you look at the components used to build the bike. Top-line WP forks and a rear shock that gives 13.5in of travel, combined with a dry weight of 154kg and power output of 53hp from the four-valve single-cylinder engine ensure impeccable off-road ability. In addition the enormous 28-litre fuel tank makes huge distances possible between refuelling stops – perfect for those long days on the trail when fuel is not readily available.

The LC4 power unit has evolved very successfully over the years, with small increases in capacity (from the original 610cc to 625cc), high-flow cylinder heads and the introduction of fuel injection, albeit for more recent road-going models.

Simple technology combined with excellent build quality makes the LC4 one of the most reliable and dependable bikes in the overlanding arena. As good as it is, though, the KTM does have its idiosyncrasies. The big single-cylinder engine vibrates quite a lot, so you need to keep an eye on fasteners and not let any come loose, and the seat height can be a little challenging for those of shorter build, but these shortcomings are more than outweighed by the overall benefits of the complete package.

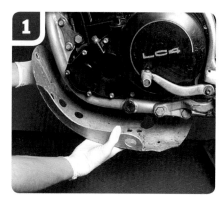

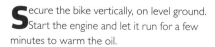

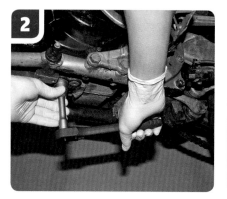

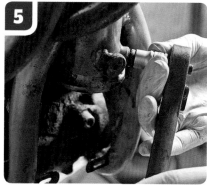

Secure the bike vertically, on level ground. Start the engine and let it run for a few minutes to warm the oil.

1. Remove the sump guard (if fitted) to get better access to the crankcase drain bolts.
2. Place a drain tray underneath the sump and undo the hex-head drain bolts. Allow the old oil to drain completely into the drain pan. Refit the oil drain bolts, preferably using new sealing washers.
3. Take care not to lose or damage the fine-mesh screen.
4. Place the drain pan underneath the chassis front down-tube and use an appropriate tool to remove the filter canister.
5. Drain the chassis front down-tube by removing the drain bolt: early models have an external drain bolt; post-2001 models have a socket head drain bolt beneath the oil filter mounting flange.
6. Allow the old oil to drain completely and re-fit the down-tube drain bolt before replacing or renewing the oil filter canister. Lubricate the canister's rubber seal with a little engine oil before fitting.
7. Tightening the oil filter canister by hand is generally sufficient; you do not usually need a tool.
8. Remove the gearbox output sprocket cover and disconnect the green neutral light switch wire.
9. Access to the secondary filter cover can sometimes be limited. Depending on the model, either remove the brake lever, or depress it and wedge it down with a screwdriver.
10. If required, disconnect the oil lines to the filter cover to aid access.

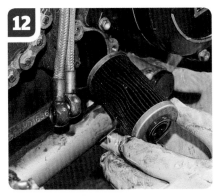

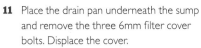

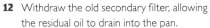

11 Place the drain pan underneath the sump and remove the three 6mm filter cover bolts. Displace the cover.

12 Withdraw the old secondary filter, allowing the residual oil to drain into the pan.

13 Install the new filter core; ensure that the open end of the filter faces outwards.

14 Inspect and replace the secondary oil filter cover 'O' ring. Replace the secondary oil filter cover and tighten the three bolts – at 5Nm these require very little tightening torque. Reconnect the oil lines if they were displaced earlier. Reconnect the neutral switch wire and replace the sprocket cover and – if removed – the brake lever.

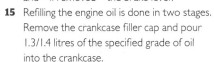

15 Refilling the engine oil is done in two stages. Remove the crankcase filler cap and pour 1.3/1.4 litres of the specified grade of oil into the crankcase.

16 Remove the filler bolt at the top of the chassis front frame tube and use a syringe or similar to fill with about 0.6 litre of the specified oil, until it flows from the hole.

17 Replace the top filler bolt using a new sealing washer where appropriate. At this stage it must be left very loose! Start the engine and let it idle for a few seconds. As soon as a dribble of oil is seen coming from the filler hole tighten the bolt and stop the engine. Ensure that the correct torque is applied to the bolt to seal and secure it properly. Wipe any excess oil off the chassis – the frame tube is now purged of air and primed. Check the crankcase oil level by screwing the dipstick all the way in and remove it again. The oil level should be between the marks on the dipstick – adjust as required. Refit the sump guard.

Air filter service

The LC4 air filter is placed conventionally underneath the saddle which makes it very simple to service. Care must be taken, however, to follow the instructions when re-oiling the foam element as overdoing it can adversely affect its air flow characteristics.

1 Remove the four screws holding the left-side air box cover.
2 Unhook the spring bar and withdraw the foam filter assembly.
3 Withdraw the filter cage from the foam filter.
4 Clean the filter or use a fresh pre-oiled filter.
5 Fit the filter cage and insert the foam filter assembly into the air box, ensuring it is seated correctly.
6 Secure the foam filter assembly with the spring bar.
7 Replace the side air box cover.

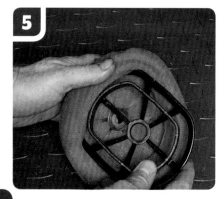

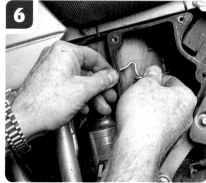

Brake service

The following procedure applies largely to both front and rear brake calipers fitted to the LC4 as they are of similar design.

1. Using hand pressure only, press the caliper against the disc to retract the pistons.
2. Remove the brake pad pin, noting the orientation of the 'R' clips for re-assembly. Withdraw the pads from the rear of the caliper.
3. Clean and check the pads, or if they are outside service limits replace them with new pads.
4. Inspect the brake pad pin and clean or replace if excessively worn.
5. Smear a little copper-based brake grease on the backs of the pads, taking care not to contaminate the braking surface.
6. Install the pads from the rear of the caliper.
7. Secure the pads with the brake pad pin and refit the 'R' clips. Actuate the brake lever several times to reseat the pads on the disc.

KTM LC8 950/990 ADVENTURE
SERVICING

When it was first introduced in 2003, the LC8 made a significant impact on the adventure motorcycle market. With heritage steeped in competition achievement, the LC8 adventure bikes were destined for success.

KTM took great steps forward, designing and creating a completely new bike from the wheels up, using technology and engineering developed for and proven in Dakar rallies in the two years prior to its launch. The KTM Adventure gets its agility from KTM's dirt-racing experience, using top-line suspension components and a tall, narrow chassis to give it true off-road ability.

The long-stroke 75° V-twin Rotax engine was engineered specifically for this bike. While it is extremely powerful, the way it delivers its motive force is perfect for the dirt, with smooth, useable power available from the first whisper of the throttle.

While the LC8's height can be initially intimidating, this aspect of the bike comes into its own when on the move. The long-travel suspension is perfectly matched to the bike, and provides an ideal compromise for road and trail. The firm suppleness of the suspension gives confidence on the tarmac and control in a wide variety of off-road conditions, and in addition the 21-inch front wheel instils unrivalled steering precision.

Fuel injection, needed for the bike to meet emission and environmental controls, was introduced in 2007. This was complemented by an increase in capacity from 950 to 990cc, giving a healthy increase in power and torque.

The bike should be thoroughly warm before performing this operation, so start the engine and leave it on idle until the fan starts to operate.

1 Release the lower engine cover by removing the four securing bolts and place to one side.

2 Place a suitable receptacle underneath the sump. Locate the oil drain bolt and loosen – take care as the engine and oil will be hot.

3 Allow the oil to drain into the tray and clear any debris off the magnetic end of the bolt. Refit the drain bolt – with a new washer/gasket if available.

4 Remove the oil filter cartridge cover.

5 Withdraw the old filter.

6 Install the new filter.

7 Refit the cover – with a new seal if available.

8 Refill the oil system from the right-hand side with fresh oil. Restart the engine and run at idle until warm. Turn off the ignition, leave for one minute then check the level again and top up as required.

9 Replace the oil filler cap securely and refit the lower engine cover.

Air filter service

The LC8 air filter housing is located on top of the engine, straddling the throttle bodies. Access to the filter itself is quite tricky and involves the removal and displacement of several key components. Take care not to lose the spring clips locating the breather hose to the spigot on the filter cover.

1 Remove the seat unit.
2 Remove the top tank cubby-hole (six self-tapping black screws) and place carefully to one side. Remove the two rearmost fuel tank securing bolts.
3 Remove the air-box air temperature sensor plug (cut the zip tie to release). Remove tank pressure balance pipe and disconnect the crankcase breather and recirculation hoses.
4 Gently displace the tank to allow access to the rear air filter cover bolts.
5 Remove cover bolts – eight in total. Lift out air-box cover to reveal the air filter element.
6 Twist off the throttle body 'trumpets' (one-eighth of a turn anti-clockwise) and place to one side.
7 Lift out the air filter element and clean with compressed air, or replace as necessary.
8 Reassemble in reverse order, not forgetting to replace the inlet trumpets as they hold the inner part of the filter.
9 Ensure that all bolts are secure and that the cubby-hole cover operates properly.

Front brake service

The LC8 990 uses a high-performance braking system designed by Brembo. There is good access to all the major components required for a brake service, and as long as there is no significant corrosion replacement of the brake pads is a straightforward affair.

1. Start by looking down the caliper to check the condition of the pads.
2. Front pads are secured by a spring-collared slider pin and 'R' clip.
3. Gently drift out the pin.
4. Release the pads.
5. Clean and lubricate the pad-retaining pin, but replace if visibly worn.
6. Refit the pads in the reverse order of disassembly.
7. Insert the pad-retaining pin – note orientation of the 'R' clip. Pump brake lever to seat pads on the disc.

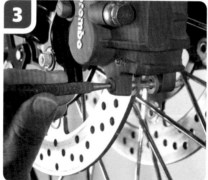

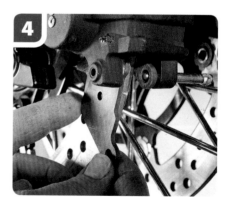

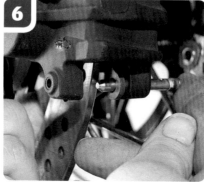

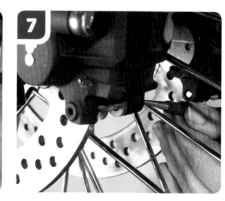

Rear brake service

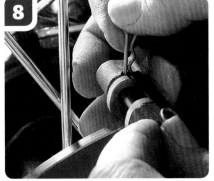

As is typical with Brembo systems, the front and rear calipers are very similar in construction and operation, so the procedure employed for the front brake can equally be applied to the rear.

1 Rear pads are secured by a pad-retaining pin and two flanged 'R' clips.
2 Remove 'R' clips to release slider pin.
3 Pull pads from the rear of the caliper.
4 Clean any dirty or corroded components.
5 Refit pads in the reverse order of disassembly.
6 Push up on the bottom edge of pad to allow the pad-retaining pin to engage.
7 Fully insert the pad-retaining pin.
8 Insert the flanged 'R' clips – note orientation on the caliper. Pump the brake pedal to seat the pads on the disc.

HONDA XRV750 AFRICA TWIN
SERVICING

Almost all motorcycle manufacturers have produced a model with overlanding pretensions and many have fallen by the wayside as nothing more than exercises in cosmetic bodywork, but very few survive to become virtual icons of their age. Honda's Africa Twin (XRV750) is one of those survivors. The bike's heritage is firmly rooted in the development of the NXR750 rally bike that took four Paris–Dakar victories in the 1980s, and it shows in the way it has endured the test of time, having achieved almost cult status among a group of dedicated owners.

The Africa Twin (AT) has an immensely capable 750cc V-twin engine which, by the end of the model's production life, had been developed to deliver some 62bhp and 46ft/lb of torque. This gives it a broad spread of useable but unintimidating power, making it an ideal power unit for an overlanding motorcycle, with the softer state of tune making it particularly robust and capable of many thousands of miles before any significant maintenance is required.

There is no doubt that, in its showroom guise, the AT is best suited for road use, but with a little work to the suspension and a suitable set of intermediate or off-road tyres it can be easily transformed into a highly capable overlanding motorcycle. The chassis is equipped with long-travel suspension to soak up the harshest of terrain and the 21-inch front wheel copes well with the demands of off-road riding. Enhanced by a redesigned seat, revised bodywork and a 23-litre fuel tank, which gives a range of over 200 miles (320km), these bikes are still in high demand, and combine an enviable record for mechanical reliability with the ability to cover considerable daily distances.

The last production year for the Africa Twin was 2003, but the bike's ability and characteristics have given it enduring appeal.

Engine oil service	78
Air filter service	79
Front brake service	80
Rear brake service	81

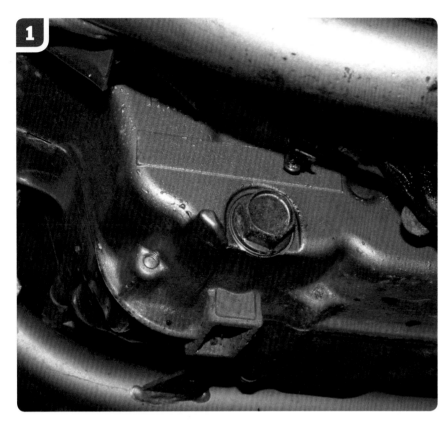

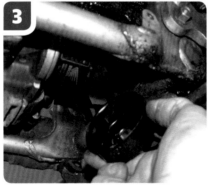

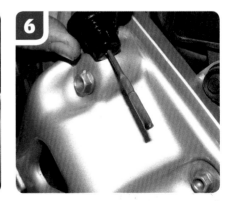

Warm the engine by running it at idle until the cooling fan comes on. Switch off, and let it stand for a few minutes to allow the oil to drain back into the sump.

1   Support the bike using the sidestand as the drain plug is on the left-hand side of the engine and this will help the oil to drain completely.
2   Place a drain tray beneath the engine and unscrew the oil drain plug. When the oil has completely drained, refit the drain plug using a new sealing washer.
3   Using an appropriate tool, remove the old filter.
4   Lubricate the new filter's seal with a little oil before installing it, using the appropriate tool and tightening it to the specified torque setting.
5   Refill the engine with the correct volume of the specified oil, checking the final level using the dipstick on the filler cap. The level should be between the upper and lower marks.
6   Refit the filler cap and run the engine for a minute or so to distribute the oil throughout the engine. Allow a few minutes for the oil to drain back into the sump before making a final dipstick check and topping up to the upper mark on the dipstick.

Air filter service

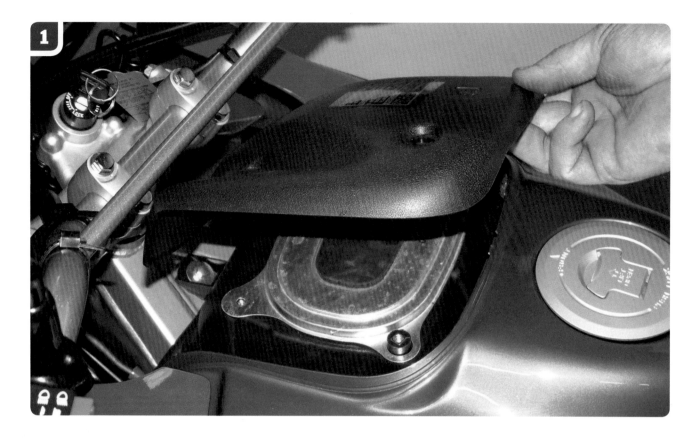

While the principle of operation is similar, some versions of the Africa Twin have slightly different location points for the air filter housing.

1 Undo the air filter cover screws, noting their locations, and remove the cover.
2 Withdraw the filter. Install the new filter, or if possible clean the old one by blowing with compressed air in the opposite direction of airflow.
3 Replace the filter cover, ensuring the correct location of the screws.

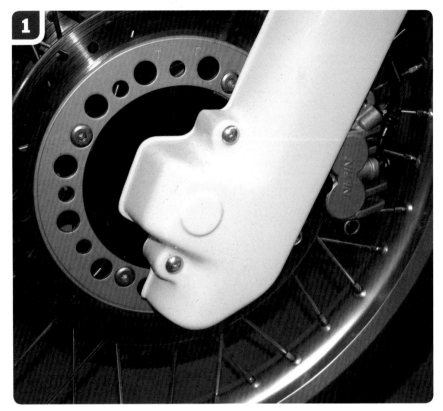

Certain models of Africa Twin utilise shields and protectors for the lower fork leg which may need to be displaced or removed to access the brake caliper. Take care when removing the pin plug in case it has corroded.

1 Remove or displace the fork guards to give better access to the brake caliper. Push the caliper against the disc to force the piston into the caliper.
2 Unscrew the brake pad-retaining pin plug from the caliper.
3 Unscrew the pad-retaining pin.
4 Withdraw the pads from the caliper and clean or replace as necessary.
5 If the pad backing shim is present, ensure it is correctly refitted before installing the pads in the caliper.
6 Ensure the 'toe' of the pad is correctly located in the caliper before replacing the pad-retaining pin. Use a little copper grease on the threads of the pin to make it easier to remove next time round.
7 Replace the pad-retaining pin plug and pump the brake lever several times to reset the pads against the disc.

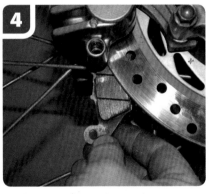

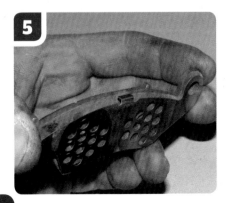

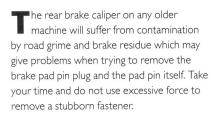

The rear brake caliper on any older machine will suffer from contamination by road grime and brake residue which may give problems when trying to remove the brake pad pin plug and the pad pin itself. Take your time and do not use excessive force to remove a stubborn fastener.

1 Push the caliper against the disc to force the piston back into the caliper to allow for the extra thickness of the new pads.
2 Remove the brake pad-retaining pin plug, and slacken the retaining pin.
3 Remove the lower caliper bolt.
4 If greater access is required, remove the brake hose clamp bolt as well.
5 Pivot the caliper upwards and remove the retaining pin before removing the brake pads. Clean or replace the pads as required, smearing a little copper-based grease on the back of each pad to help prevent brake squeal.
6 Install the pads and insert the pad pin, tightening it finger tight. Swing the caliper back down on to the disc, keeping the pads in position.
7 Ensure that the 'toe' of the pad is correctly located in the caliper.
8 Use a suitable non-permanent locking compound on the caliper bolt threads and tighten to the correct torque setting.
9 Tighten the pin pad securely and install the pin pad plug, using a little copper grease to assist future removal. Pump the brake lever several times to reset the pads against the surface of the disc.

YAMAHA XT660Z TÉNÉRÉ
SERVICING

The Yamaha Ténéré series of bikes have been at the forefront of lightweight overland motorcycling for many years. Developed from the iconic **XT500** trail bike of the early 1980s, the Ténéré has earned a well-deserved reputation of its own for being a reliable and almost unburstable workhorse.

The Yamaha **XT600Z** Ténéré was first presented in 1983, with a relatively simple 600cc four-stroke engine producing around 43hp. What set it apart was undoubtedly its then-unique 'Desert Racing' style with disc brakes, long-travel suspension and a huge 30-litre fuel tank.

The IVJ variant of the Ténéré was introduced in 1986. Benefitting from the development of the factory Rally bike, larger valves and a modified carburation system, power output rose to 46hp. The introduction of an electric starter certainly made it a lot easier to start!

In 1988 the third-generation 3AJ series came closer to the specification of factory Rally bikes, with a frame-mounted fairing and twin headlamps. Engine developments included a modified cylinder head and an improved cooling system. Braking was uprated with the fitment of a disc brake on the rear wheel.

The birth of the modern Ténéré came in 1991 following a 'wheels-up' redesign of the whole concept. Undoubtedly moving away from the Rally Replica, a completely revised chassis with reduced suspension travel gave it a much more road-biased riding style. The old air-cooled motor was replaced with a technologically advanced five-valve liquid-cooled engine, guaranteeing minimal maintenance and improved environmental friendliness. This model received a cosmetic redesign in 1994, with the fitment of a streamlined twin-lamp fairing based on the **XTZ750 Super Ténéré**.

The soft and civilised '94 Ténéré was the last big single-cylinder trail bike offered by Yamaha until the new **XT660Z** Ténéré exploded into the marketplace in 2008. Sharp styling combined with cutting-edge engine technologies and a very capable chassis have ensured that this incarnation of the Ténéré will stay at the head of the field for many years.

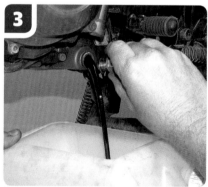

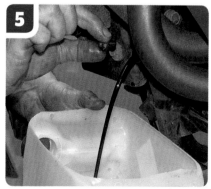

This operation should be performed with a warm engine – start the bike and allow it to idle until the cooling fan operates. Switch off and leave the bike for five minutes to allow the oil to return to the sump.

1   Secure the bike vertically on level ground. Unscrew the oil filler cap to vent the crankcase and allow oil to flow freely.
2   Remove the sump guard and place a drain tray underneath the crankcase drain plug.
3   Undo the crankcase drain plug and allow the sump to empty into the drain tray – remember the oil will still be hot.
4   Refit the crankcase drain plug using a new sealing washer and tighten to the recommended torque.
5   Unscrew the oil tank drain bolt at the front of the engine and allow it to drain completely before refitting the bolt using a new sealing washer if required. Torque to the recommended figure.

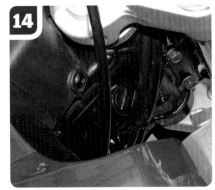

6 If you are replacing the oil filter, remove the filter housing drain bolt and allow the oil to drain completely.

7 Undo the filter housing bolts and remove the cover to access the filter.

8 Remove O-rings from the cover and drain bolt hole – replace using new sealing rings where possible.

9 Fit a new oil filter with the rubber end facing out.

10 Replace the filter housing cover and tighten the bolts, including the filter housing drain bolt.

11 The engine oil must be added in two stages (check your manual for volumes). After adding the first stage, replace the oil filler cap then start the engine and gently 'blip' the throttle five or six times. Turn off the engine and wait for five minutes before adding the second stage of oil. If you have renewed the filter you may need slightly more oil.

12 Check that the oil circuit is completely full by starting the engine and letting it idle while loosening the check bolt on top of the oil filter housing. Oil should seep past the threads.

13 If no seepage is seen after one minute, stop the engine and investigate, draining and refilling the oil if necessary. If all is well, allow the engine to idle for a few minutes then check the final level using the oil tank dipstick, and add or remove oil until the correct level is reached.

14 Refit and tighten the oil filler cap.

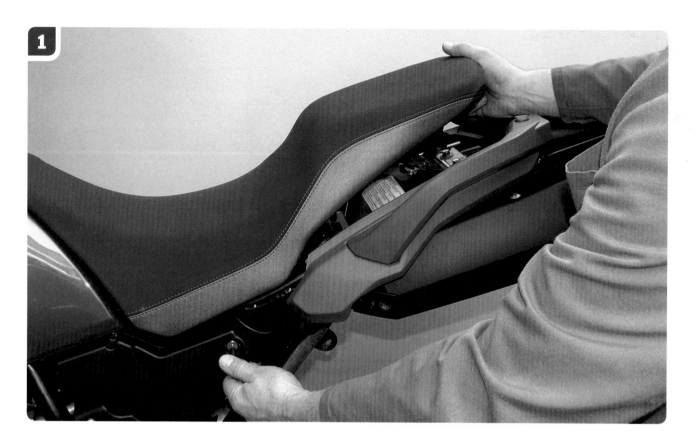

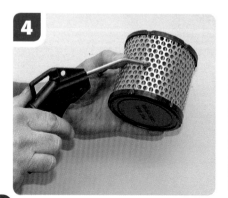

The XT660Z utilises a conventional rigid paper element filter mounted in an air box underneath the seat. Other than the removal of the seat, no significant disassembly is required to change or clean the air filter canister.

1   Remove the seat to access the air duct cover.
2   Undo the air duct screws and remove the cover.
3   Withdraw the filter element.
4   If the filter is not damaged and simply dusty, it can be blown clear with compressed air; otherwise replace it with a new filter. If required, clean the inside of the air box with a lightly oiled cloth, then install the filter.
5   Replace the air duct cover, ensuring the filter is correctly seated, and then refit the seat unit.

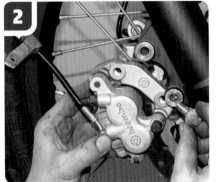

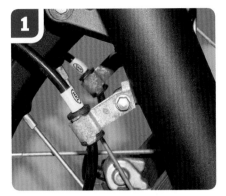

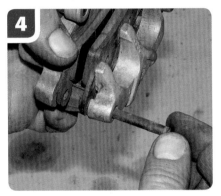

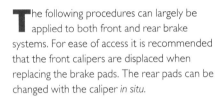

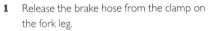

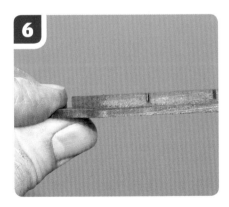

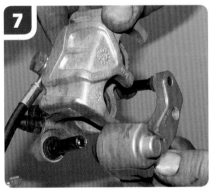

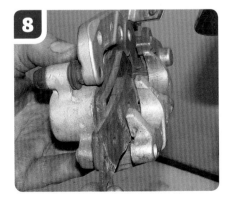

The following procedures can largely be applied to both front and rear brake systems. For ease of access it is recommended that the front calipers are displaced when replacing the brake pads. The rear pads can be changed with the caliper *in situ*.

1   Release the brake hose from the clamp on the fork leg.
2   Unscrew the caliper-mounting bolts and slide the caliper off the disc.
3   Remove the 'R' clips.
4   Remove the pad-retaining pin.
5   Release the pads from the caliper.
6   Check the condition of the pads, and clean or replace as necessary.
7   The XT660Z uses a twin-piston sliding caliper design – if the caliper does not move smoothly slide the caliper off the mounting bracket. Clean off all traces of corrosion and old hardened grease from the slider pins and their rubber boots. Apply a smear of silicone-based grease to the boots and pins before reassembly.
8   Apply a smear of copper brake grease to the back of the pad before reinstalling in the caliper. Clean the pad-retaining pin and lubricate it with a small amount of copper grease. Reinstall the pad pin and the 'R' clips.
9   Slide the calipers back on to the disc and locate in place with the mounting bolts. Tighten the caliper-mounting bolts to the specified torque figure, and reattach the hose clamp on the forkleg. When both calipers have been remounted, pump the brake lever several times to reseat the pads on the disc and verify proper operation of the braking system before riding.

Touratech

GENERIC SERVICING

t might come as a bit of a surprise, but even today most motorcycles are essentially very similar to each other. Admittedly, some manufacturers use advanced computer-controlled technologies, or special tools to perform certain tasks on some specific components, but beyond that the principles of a motorcycle are just about the same the world over. Brakes, wheels, tyres, nuts and bolts, filters, levers and lights; these are just a few of the more basic and commonly found components and systems of a motorcycle.

In this modern age of consumerism and convenience it is all too easy to leave virtually every aspect of your motorcycle's maintenance to a dealer, but the comfort of a credit card and a global recovery service is of no use whatsoever if a simple problem has left you stranded on the side of a dusty track miles from civilisation. What works in these situations is knowing what to do and having the confidence to do it. Possessing a few basic skills and a little knowledge could save you more than just the inconvenience of a trip to your local dealer; indeed in more extreme circumstances it could potentially save your life if you hit a problem while travelling in a remote part of the world.

This chapter covers a few of the basic tasks that can be achieved on your bike, both while at home or during a tour, and usually with only a modest selection of tools.

Drive chain servicing

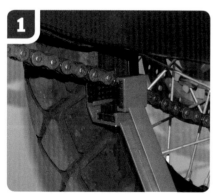

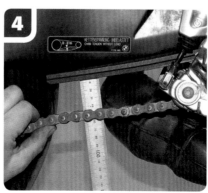

Drive chains need regular maintenance to keep them in the best condition. Keeping the chain clean, lubricated and properly adjusted is the key to long life and efficient function.

1 With the bike on the centre stand and the real wheel off the ground, use a clean stiff brush to remove the worst of any dirt and debris from the chain and sprockets. A rag soaked in paraffin will do a good job of cleaning the chain, but take care not to contaminate the tyre or brake components. Dry the chain with another cloth or a blast of compressed air.

2 Check for chain wear by trying to lift the chain off the rear sprocket – if you can lift it by more than 3–4mm it will need replacing.

3 Inspect the sprockets for wear at the same time – if the teeth are hooked or excessively worn then they too will need replacing.

4 The chain slack can be checked by pushing the chain upwards at the middle of the lower run. Look in the bike's handbook to see if it needs to be checked while on the centre stand, or with the wheels on the ground (it does make a difference!).

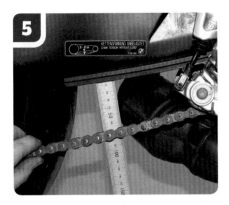

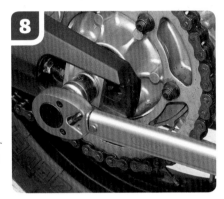

5   Roll the bike or turn the wheel until the chain is at its tightest point on the bottom run, then check that the deflection falls within the specification given in the owner's manual. If the difference between tight and slack spots on the chain is significant, then the chain has stretched unevenly and will need replacing.

6   A chain that is too tight can accelerate wear and potentially damage the gearbox output shaft bearing (in the crankcases behind the engine sprocket). If it is too loose then there is a real danger that it could jump off the sprockets altogether. Adjust the slack by loosening the rear axle nut, then loosen the adjustment screw locknuts.

7   Use the adjustment bolts to move the axle either backwards or forwards to achieve the correct range of slack in the middle of the bottom chain run. Be sure that both adjusters are moved the same distance by checking their position on the index marks stamped into the swing arm.

8   Once you are happy that all is properly adjusted, tighten the adjustment bolt locknuts, followed by the axle nut, to the torque specifications given in your owner's handbook. Do a final check of the chain's free tension.

9   Lubricate the chain with an approved lubricant. Check your owner's manual for the manufacturer's recommendation. In general terms all major lubricant suppliers have a chain lube available.

10 When applying the lube, concentrate on the inside faces of the link plates, as the lube will penetrate deep into the rollers from that point. Be careful not to overspray on to the brake disc and tyre as the excess will be very hard to clean off.

Drive chain removal and fitting

The articulated roller transmission chain – or drive chain – is the flexible link between the bike's engine and its rear wheel. It might look simple but it is actually manufactured to extremely high tolerances and is expected to perform flawlessly in a very hostile environment with sporadic lubrication to keep things moving smoothly. Knowing how to look after a chain and how to repair it when necessary is an essential skill.

1 Identify the chain's 'soft link', it is usually the one with a dimple on the rivet head.
2 Use an appropriately sized chain tool to push the pin through the chain side plates.
3 Separate the chain and remove the remaining link pin.
4 Withdraw the link, and keep the redundant 'O' rings as spares if they are reuseable.

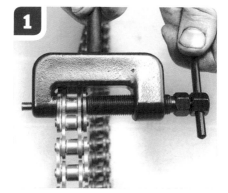

5

6

7

8

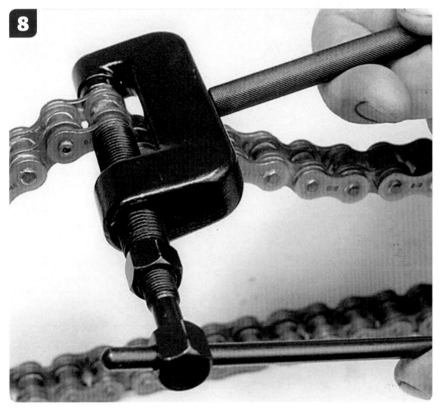

5   Install the new link, remembering to use the new 'O' rings and a liberal smear of chain grease on the link pins.

6   Offer up the new link's side plate and partially install it on the link pins.

7   Fit the appropriate anvil to the chain tool to press the link plate on to the link pins.

8   Remove the anvil and install the riveting pin into the chain tool. Tighten the tool over the head of the new link pin to spread it and lock it into place.

9   The finished result should look like this. Do not over-tighten the rivet as it will cause the link to bind and cause a permanent tight spot in the chain, greatly increasing its wear rate.

10 A spring link can usually be used in place of a 'soft link', but be sure that you have adequate clearance for the extra width of the spring clip. The spring clip *must* be installed with its closed end facing the direction of the chain's travel.

9

10

Cooling system servicing

Visual inspection

The cooling system of a modern motorcycle is often overlooked as it is almost a passive component. With time, however, certain parts of the system will deteriorate and require attention, usually as a result of failure or leakage. The nature of the system means that it will need to be cool before it is inspected, and drained before any work can be done on it. Most automotive coolants are toxic when ingested so levels of care must be taken when handling it, and disposal restrictions may apply in your area so check with your local authority for further information.

1   Check the coolant level in the expansion tank, which will generally be at the side of the bike, possibly tucked behind a body panel – the level should be between the MIN and MAX marks. Top up with fresh coolant as required.
2   Check the coolant level in the radiator by removing the pressure cap – there should be sufficient coolant in the radiator to completely cover the core. Top up with fresh coolant as required.
3   Check the condition of the hoses. They should not have any signs of abrasion, cracking or wear, and when squeezed should feel firm and resilient, not soft or rubbery.
4   Inspect the clamps securing the hoses to the engine casings, ensuring they are tight and show no signs of coolant seepage.

Draining and replacing coolant

Check your owner's manual to identify the preferred method and location of the relevant drain screws or bolts. Some models will simply require the disconnection of the lower radiator hose.

1 Remove the top radiator cap then drain and collect the old coolant and store ready for disposal. Drain any coolant from the expansion tank.
2 If the old coolant is excessively dirty or discoloured, flush the entire system with fresh water. Disconnect the lower radiator hose and insert a hosepipe into the filler neck of the radiator. Allow fresh water to run through the system until it flows cleanly and freely.
3 Refit the hoses, ensuring that all clamps are tightly fixed, and refill the system with fresh coolant of an appropriate concentration/ protection level for your area.
4 Start the engine and allow the bike to idle for a few minutes to circulate the coolant. Stop the engine and carefully remove the radiator filler cap – do not forget to depressurise the system gradually – and top up the level if necessary. Fill the expansion tank with fresh coolant to a level midway between the MIN and MAX marks. Check with your owner's handbook for bleeding points to release any trapped air and bleed if required.
5 Restart the engine, and allow it to idle until it reaches full operating temperature. Turn it off and allow it to cool before making a final check on coolant levels, topping up as required.

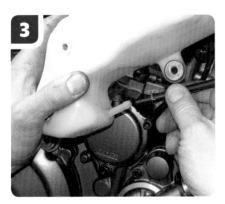

Cooling system servicing

Replacing a cooling hose

1 Drain the system as detailed in the previous procedure.

2 Release the hose clamps and remove the old hose. If it has never been removed before it may be stuck and need to be cut off the spigot.

3 Install the hose clamps over the new hose, and push it on to the spigots. New hoses can be quite stiff and can be softened a little by soaking them in hot water before installation. Install the hose clamps in the correct place, ensuring that they are oriented correctly. Some manufacturers fit spring-type hose clamps, but these can be replaced with worm-drive clamps or 'jubilee' clips if preferred, but remember to check them periodically.

4 Refill the system as described in the previous procedure.

Control cables

Control cables (Bowden cables) are a simple way of transmitting pulling forces from one place to another, but the greatest enemies of the humble cable are friction and corrosion. Some cables have a self-lubricating nylon or PTFE liner which reduces the drag of the cable but others will require oil or grease to keep them running smoothly and corrosion-free.

1 Wind the cable adjuster in completely to release the tension on the cable. Align the slots on the adjuster and release the cable from the lever. Check the condition of the cable, looking for frayed strands or signs of corrosion.

2 This simple device uses the pressure of the aerosol to lubricate the length of the cable.

3 Alternatively, cut the finger from a rubber glove to make an oil reservoir, letting gravity take the oil where it is needed. If your cable has a liner, a liberal smear of grease will prevent corrosion where the cable is exposed.

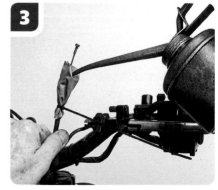

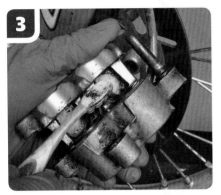

If you have used your bike over a typical European winter, then there is a very good chance that the brake pistons may be dirty or caked in road grime and this may prevent them retracting fully into the caliper, causing brake drag. This overheats the brakes and will rapidly wear out the pads, to say nothing of the extra fuel that will be wasted.

1   Remove the caliper from the fork leg. If you have small wheel rims you may need to remove the wheel first. Remove the brake pads and – if necessary – place a tyre lever or a slim piece of wood between the pistons.

2   Gently pump the brake lever or pedal until the pistons just start to emerge from the caliper, and clamp the lever to prevent accidental ejection.

3   CAUTION! Use an aerosol brake cleaner to flood out any debris from around the pistons. Do *not* blow any dust out as there may still be an asbestos component used in the pads. Use a toothbrush soaked in a little brake fluid to scrub any deposits off the exposed part of the piston/s.

4   Finish with a strip of rag to wipe the piston surfaces clean and remove any excess brake fluid.

5   If the caliper is a sliding type rather than an an opposed-piston design, clean the slider pin with brake cleaner and use fine emery cloth or wet and dry paper to remove any compacted debris or corrosion on the pin.

6   Push the pistons back into the caliper. Refit the brake pads using a small amount of copper-based brake grease on the back of the pad to prevent brake squeal, and a small amount on the slider pin, not forgetting to reinstall the 'R' clips. CAUTION! Be extremely careful not to get any grease on the friction material of the pad or the face of the disc. Use copious amounts of brake cleaner and clean rag to deal with any mishaps.

7   Refit the caliper to the fork leg and refit the wheel, if it was removed. Pump the brake lever or pedal to set the pads on the disc and check the brake action.

Brake fluid replacement/bleeding

Heavy or constant braking can generate great amounts of heat in the calipers. If the brake fluid is contaminated with absorbed water (see pages 33–34 regarding brake fluid's hygroscopic nature), this heat will cause the water to vaporise, creating vapour bubbles in the fluid. These pockets of gas will almost completely disable the system, as all the effort you put into squeezing the brake lever is actually used to compress the gas bubbles, preventing any significant braking force reaching the disc and making the brake lever or pedal feel very spongy, with a corresponding reduction in brake effectiveness. The solution involves replacing the fluid and consequently purging any residual air or contaminated fluid from the brake system.

This can be a fiddly task, and is often better achieved with either an assistant or a brake-bleeding kit.

■ CAUTION! Brake fluid is extremely damaging to paintwork and some plastics so great care must be taken to prevent spills or splashes. Any fluid that does get on to the bike's bodywork must be wiped off immediately with a clean cloth.

■ Only ever use clean, fresh brake fluid from an unopened bottle, and refit the brake fluid reservoir cap as soon as the job has been done to reduce the possibility of water vapour contamination.

■ Used brake fluid should be treated in the same way as used engine oil and disposed of at an approved recycling facility. Use rubber or vinyl gloves when using brake fluid, and wash with soap and water as soon as practical should you get it on to your skin.

ABS WARNING

If your bike has anti-lock braking (ABS) then confirm with your dealer whether intervention will be required to reset the bike's main computer – some bikes with a combination of servo-assistance and ABS require a specific signal to be sent to the ABS pump to purge the lines. This can only be done with main dealer equipment.

Thorvaldur Örn Kristmundsson

KTM UK Ltd.

Conventional bleeding

1. Locate and identify the bleed valve on the top of the brake caliper.

2. Loosen using a ring spanner and attach a length of clear plastic hose to the valve – clear windscreen washer hose is perfect – and put the other end into a suitable receptacle below the level of the caliper.

3. Tighten the bleed valve until it just seats in the caliper, fill the brake fluid reservoir and prime the master cylinder by pumping it gently.

4. Gently squeeze the brake lever at the same time as opening the bleed valve, but tighten the bleed valve *before* releasing the lever. This pushes fresh fluid into the brake line and tightening the valve prevents it being sucked back into the reservoir.

5. Repeat the process, progressively filling the system with clean fluid as the old fluid is purged out. Take care not to let the level in the reservoir get too low and top up as required, otherwise air will be sucked into the line and the whole process will have to be started afresh.

6. When you see brake fluid emerging in the clear hose you will see that it contains lots of bubbles. Repeat the process until *all* bubbles have disappeared and clean, clear fluid is all that is in the clear hose.

7. Tighten the bleed valve and replace the dust cap, then pump the lever several times to set the pads against the disc. If the lever still feels spongy then there is air trapped in the system and it will need to be purged. If the brake line has a convoluted route, the lever/reservoir unit might need to be removed and held above the handlebars to allow any trapped air bubbles a straight run through the hose, and the bleeding process repeated.

8. Troublesome air bubbles can often be purged by tying the lever back against the grip and leaving it overnight. These 'micro' bubbles will consolidate and migrate to the top of the line where they will be sucked back into the upper reservoir as the lever is released.

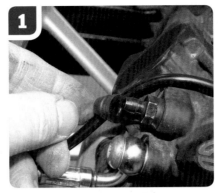

Brake fluid replacement/bleeding

Using a bleeding kit

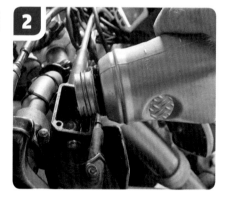

1 Attach the kit's hose to the bleed valve on the caliper and loosen the bleed valve.

2 Turn the handlebars so that the reservoir is horizontal and fill to the maximum mark with clean, fresh brake fluid.

3 Gently pump the brake lever through its full travel – you do not need to close the caliper bleed valve as the bleeding kit has a non-return valve which prevents any fluid being sucked back up the line into the reservoir.

4 Pump the brake lever until clear, bubble-free brake fluid is seen in the clear bleed pipe, making sure that the fluid level in the reservoir is kept topped up and does not fall below the minimum level.

5 Tighten the caliper bleed valve and pump the brake lever to seat the pads on to the disc, repeating the process if the brake action still feels spongy. If your bike has a twin-disc set-up the filling/bleeding procedure is the same for the second brake line.

Brake line replacement

Hydraulic brakes work on the principle of an incompressible fluid transferring the force applied to the brake lever or pedal to the brake caliper, which in turn squeezes the brake pads on to the disc. There are several factors which can severely compromise the performance of your brakes. The composition of older-style rubber brake lines can break down with age and become slightly elastic. If this happens, some of the effort you put into squeezing the brake lever or pedal will be wasted on expanding the brake line rather than squeezing the pads on to the brake disc, greatly reducing the braking effect.

You must also bleed the braking circuit to purge any trapped air out of the system following the installation of new brake lines.

1   Remove the brake fluid reservoir cap and syringe out the fluid into a suitable container.
2   Loosen and release the lower banjo bolt from the caliper, placing the end of the hose into a suitable receptacle to collect the fluid.
3   Cover any paintwork with a cloth, then release the top banjo bolt, allowing the residual fluid to flow into the receptacle.
4   Note the orientation of the banjo connectors and install the new hose in the same way.
5   Fit new copper washers to the banjo bolt and install the hose, tightening the banjo bolts to the appropriate torque figure given in the manual.
6   Refill the brake lines and reservoir with fresh brake fluid and bleed the system of any trapped air.

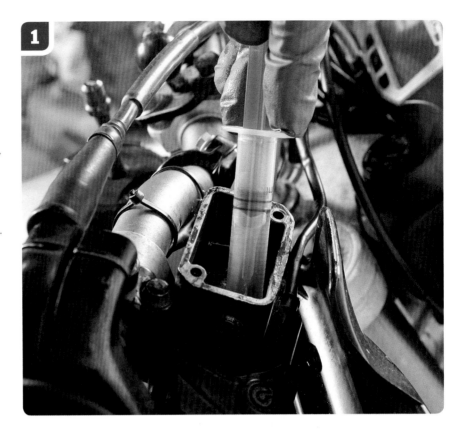

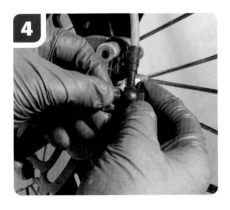

Wheel bearing replacement

Wheel bearings are components with a very variable life – some bearing/wheel/bike combinations can last many thousands of miles, while others only last for what seems like a matter of weeks. Without doubt, a significant factor in bearing failure will be the quality of the original equipment items, and some manufacturers will not always fit top-line bearings, so these will ultimately suffer premature failure. If not seen to, a bearing failure can at best make the bike's handling challenging, and at worst can seriously damage the wheel hub, so if you are planning long overland distances, it will pay dividends to take – and be able to fit – spare bearings.

When purchasing bearings, you should ideally have the old ones for comparison. Otherwise, check with your service manual or parts list for the bearing's dimensions – inside diameter, outside diameter and thickness. Make sure that the new bearings are sealed at both faces for maximum protection.

Replacing bearings is relatively easy, and can be achieved with a surprisingly simple selection of tools – drift rod, hammer and circlip pliers (if circlips are fitted).

1. Remove the wheel
2. Check for seals and bearing-retaining circlips and remove them if fitted.
3. Working from one side, use the drift rod and hammer through the hub to gently knock the opposite bearing out of its seat. You may need to lever the inner bearing spacer to one side to get the drift on to an edge of the inner race of the bearing.
4. Work 'around the clock' to be sure that the bearing remains square as it is pushed out. If the bearing starts to tip in its seat, correct it by simply tapping on the opposite side. The bearing should pop out quite readily once it starts to move.
5. Remove the bearing spacer if it has not already dropped free, and turn the wheel over to repeat the operation on the opposite bearing. Remove any traces of old grease or dirt that may stop the new bearing seating correctly.
6. When introducing the new bearing take great care to keep it square. If it is allowed to tip it will make it impossible to install, and forcing it will cause damage to the wheel hub. An easy-to-use tool can be made from a length of threaded rod, two nuts and a couple of large washers.
7. If you don not have a tool, then some heat will help. Try putting a wad of cloth over the hub and pour boiling water over it. The cloth will hold the heat from the water exactly where it is needed to make the hub expand enough to be able to slip the bearing in with minimal effort.
8. When seating the new bearing *do not hammer the inner race*! This will cause irreparable damage to the bearing, and will considerably reduce its working life. Use a spreader or a large socket with the same diameter as the outer race and tap it gently home.
9. Refit the retaining circlip (if fitted).
10. When the first bearing is located properly, turn the wheel over, insert the bearing spacer tube and repeat the installation process for the second bearing. Tap the bearing home until the spacer tube is a sliding fit between the inner races.
11. Refit the bearing circlip (if fitted).
12. Refit the wheel, paying particular attention to the order of spacers and bearing covers, and of course the final tightening of all nuts and fasteners.

part from the actual planning of your tour, perhaps the most daunting task, especially if it is your first time, is preparing your bike for the journey that lies ahead and having the confidence that it will actually do what you ask of it. This confidence comes from the knowledge that your bike has been looked after as it should, that any consumable components such as brake discs will have the maximum life possible, and that any accessory has been properly fitted.

There is no single bike that is 'journey ready' out of the crate. The list of potential modifications that can be made to a modern ADV bike is almost endless – you only have to look in any of the accessory manufacturers' catalogues to see pages and pages of equipment that can be attached to your motorcycle. There is no doubt that some are quite functional, some even essential, but a lot can simply be expensive trinkets and gadgets that do no more than offer a distraction.

There is a raft of opinion on how a bike – any bike – should be prepared for a tour, but at the end of the day you are the rider and therefore you must determine what is needed. Understanding your bike and knowing your own limits are two of the most important factors. It is very easy to get carried away with preparing the bike in readiness for the worst possible eventuality, but with a little care and forethought you can avoid many of the problems that often take the under-prepared rider by surprise.

Once you have taken the time to examine your route and look at the terrain you are likely to encounter, you can start making relevant decisions about the accessories you will need, then go about finding them and fitting them. It is very easy to create a 'shopping list' of many items which could cost a great deal of money, so try to have your budget figure in mind and really prioritise your list of needs and wants.

Once you have bought an accessory, compare it with the OE (original equipment) component to see where the differences are and take the time to look at it and see what it does and how it works. It is really worthwhile taking the time to fit the accessory yourself, too, as it will offer you an insight into how it interacts with the rest of the motorcycle as well as giving you a chance to 'get a feel' of working on the bike.

The 'go anywhere' concept of the modern ADV motorcycle almost encourages the assumption that it is the ideal motorcycle for any rider. Nothing could be further from the truth! Just as there is no single 'average' person, there is no single 'ideal' ADV bike. An ADV bike should have a degree of adjustability to accommodate the differences in body shape of a reasonable proportion of riders, with seats that can be adjustable for height, handlebars that can be rotated in their mountings, adjustable control levers and sometimes even adjustable footrests. Take the time to learn how all of these variables can be adjusted to best suit you.

If you find yourself stooping while standing on the footrests, try rotating the bars in their mounting to get a little more height or reach. If this does not work for you, try fitting handlebar risers, which can lift the bars by as much as 30mm; some also offer a rearward shift which will help anyone with a shorter back. It is critical to make sure that operation cables or hydraulic lines are not overstretched in a new position as this would be a serious compromise to safety. If this is the case, rerouting the cables can sometimes solve the problem. Otherwise, extended items can usually be sourced from a specialist provider. Do not forget that lowering the seat has the same effect as raising the bars while seated, so check to see if it is adjustable. If there is no

adjustment, then 'off-the-shelf' lowered or sculpted seats are available. If you need the seat to fit you personally, there are specialist remanufacturers who can disassemble your unit and re-engineer your seat pad by either reprofiling or fitting a pressure-relief pad. Once the desired result has been achieved, the seat is re-covered according to your needs.

Check that the reach required to operate the brake and clutch levers is comfortably within your finger span and adjust as required. If you cannot adjust for reach, then replacement levers with an accentuated 'dog-leg' are available for most bikes.

Suspension adjustment

Certain components of an ADV bike are used to their maximum capacity, and most notably suspension components will come at the top of that list. When the bike is loaded and used on gravel tracks or rough surfaces, the suspension has to work constantly and consistently, and quite possibly at the top end of its designed performance range. In these extreme conditions the slightest weakness or a worn component can rapidly be taken to the point of failure, although this need not necessarily be as obvious as an oil leak from a weeping seal. When worked hard, the constant and uneven compression and extension of springs can cause them to weaken or fatigue, leading to a reduction in both their length and their responsiveness. This is known as sagging. Over time, the oil-based damping fluid can itself lose its viscosity, greatly reducing its damping properties. Some rear shock units use pressurised nitrogen to assist the steel springs, and if this leaks then the overall spring rate is greatly reduced, which may even allow the unit to compress completely or 'bottom out' under load. Checking that the suspension performs as it should is fairly simple and a lot can be learned by following a few simple procedures.

First and foremost, consult your bike's manual. The basic settings for the suspension will be listed, and unless you are happy with your existing settings, this will be the ideal place to start. From this base setting, the ideal situation is for the suspension to be set so that it uses around a third of its travel when loaded with luggage and rider. You might find that the motorcycle 'sags' outside these limits on the OE settings, so increase the unit's pre-load setting until the required parameters have been reached. If you cannot achieve a consistent and suitable range of adjustment, you may have to consider having the suspension rebuilt, with different springs to suit your needs.

Without doubt, dust and dirt are a suspension unit's worst enemy, quickly ruining seals and causing leaks, or in extreme cases causing wear on the fork legs or the shock absorber's damper rod. Protecting these components is relatively easy and very cost-effective, and could save you a lot of trouble later. Fork legs can be protected by a simple neoprene 'sock' or a concertina-style gaiter, although fitting one of these might require the fork legs to be dropped out of the steering yoke. The rear suspension components are very exposed to road grime and debris thrown up by the rear wheel. If you are not planning any serious off-roading, then a hugger will provide a great degree of protection not only to the suspension, but to the whole of the underside of the bike too. The downside of huggers is that if they fit too close to the tyre, they can quickly become clogged with mud or other debris which could then lock up the wheel.

The front wheel can be vulnerable to clogging as well, so if possible raise the front mudguard too – some motorcycles have alternative mounting points pre-cast in the bottom yoke for the fitting of a high-level Rally-style fender, which will remove this risk completely. Check your front brake lines too; some bikes use a single-line system with a 'horseshoe' line which loops over the fender to connect the calipers. If you are fitting a high-level fender then this will need to be changed as a matter of course.

This modification should be considered in any event: if you are unlucky enough to break a front fender mount, the secondary brake line immediately becomes very vulnerable and it could, in extreme circumstances, get caught in the tyre's tread pattern, locking the front wheel. There are kits available to replace the secondary line with primary lines serving each brake caliper.

⬆ **Riding on softer surfaces requires a different technique...**
📷 Joe Pichler

⬅ **Here the loss of the fender could have contributed to the fork seal's failure.**
📷 Adam Lewis

➜ Modern 'upside-down' forks are strong and reliable.
📷 Author

Steering

Steering dampers have largely been ignored by ADV motorcycle manufacturers, but take a look at almost any bike prepared for arduous conditions or difficult terrain and you will often find a steering damper fitted. A steering damper effectively increases the turning resistance of the steering, and is useful in situations where the front wheel might be subject to sudden changes in direction. When riding off-road and in more extreme conditions, for example riding in deep sand or through ruts where the front wheel can easily be deflected, the steering damper comes into its own by helping to keep the steering straight and your course true.

Any motorcycle can suffer from various degrees of 'wobble' that manifests itself as a rapid oscillation of the handlebars. Under normal riding conditions this wobble is unobtrusive and goes largely unnoticed by the rider, as the pressure put on the handlebars is sufficient to damp it out, but under certain conditions it can become much more vigorous and in the worst case can cause a loss of control of the bike. A loaded ADV bike with a tall but skinny front wheel is particularly vulnerable to wobble, especially at speed on tarmac. Stability of the front wheel is essential in every situation, and a damper helps maintain this control.

➜ With the front wheel off the ground, attempt to push and pull on the lower fork legs – worn steering-head bearings will be obvious in this test.

➜➜ Typical rim damage caused by high-speed impact. Check the wheels periodically for side-to-side and vertical deviations.

STEERING-HEAD BEARINGS

RIM DEFLECTIONS

📷 Haynes

Wheels

The wheels of your bike will take considerable levels of abuse when riding in extreme conditions so it makes a lot of sense to be sure that they are in top condition. Bearings and spokes are easy to check according to the type of wheel you have. The first check must be visual: both types of wheel must run true – they should be straight and perfectly circular. This is easily checked with the bike on the main stand: simply make sure that the wheel is off the ground and spin it – any wobbles or dents in the rim will be immediately obvious. The main defects to look for will be dips in the rim caused by hitting either a boulder or a kerb, horizontal run-out or buckling, and vertical run-out. If you have spoked wheels, any moderate deflections of the wheel rims can be pulled back 'into true' by tightening or manipulating the spokes. If the wheel cannot be brought back into true, then the rim will probably need replacing – seek a competent wheel builder for this task! Cast wheels present a slightly different set of problems. They will still suffer the same nature of damage, but again there are specialist engineers who can repair and re-true the wheel if the damage is not too severe.

Other than being at the end of their service life, wheel bearings will normally only fail from lack of lubrication. If your bike has done more than a few thousand miles it is well worth checking their condition and replacing them, if necessary. This is easily done at the same time as checking for 'trueness', as described previously. If you have the wheel off the bike for any reason, take a moment or two to turn the bearings with your finger to feel for any roughness: this will be very apparent and easily identified.

Starting with the front, get the bike on the centre stand and make sure the front wheel is off the ground – you may need help to hold the back of the bike down to do this. Turn the forks to full lock, then hold the wheel in the 'half-past-six' position and push with one hand and pull with the other. If you can feel the wheel rocking about the spindle, then the bearings are worn and will need replacing. While the wheel is off the ground, you can also check the steering head bearings for wear. Sit or kneel in front of the bike and hold the bottom of the fork legs with both hands. With the steering straight, try to push and pull the forks backwards and forwards. You should not feel any movement at all, but if you do then the steering head bearings are worn and will need replacing.

Turning your attention to the rear, again the wheel needs to be off the ground to allow for the checks. Using the same method as for the front wheel, try to rock the wheel on the spindle to feel for any movement in the bearing. If you feel or hear something knocking, then the bearing has failed and will need replacing. With the rear wheel off the ground you can also check the condition of the swing-arm pivot bearing or bush. Again, this is easier with the brake applied. Kneel or squat at the side of the bike and take the rearmost part of the wheel. Try to pull and push it from side to side – any wear will be felt or heard as a small knock as the swing-arm spindle rocks in the bushing.

WHEEL BEARINGS

SWING-ARM BEARINGS

← Side-to-side pressure at the end of the swing arm will reveal any play in the bearings.

←← With the wheel off the ground turn the handlebars to full lock so you have something solid to push against. Push and pull at the top and bottom of the wheel – any play will be apparent.

TYRE OPTIONS

■ Road tyres
Tarmac/asphalt-biased, narrow rain grooves, excellent performance on tarred roads but not suitable off-road.

■ Intermediates
70/30 road/off-road mix, wide rain grooves and big tread blocks, good road performance and adequate for use on compacted trails/gravel roads.

■ Semi-knobbly
50/50 road/off-road mix. Much better off-road performance at the cost of limited road grip and comfort.

■ Off-road/enduro
Excellent off-road performance for smaller bikes. Widely spaced, aggressive tread blocks work well on loose surfaces, but not suitable for large bikes or long tarmac journeys.

⬇ **Some punctures just can't be fixed!**
📷 ADVRider.com

Tyres

Tyres will generally be chosen to suit the kind of journey you are planning, but do give thought to the distances you will be travelling – intermediate or semi-knobbly tyres will not last as long as a more road-biased tyre, so if your journey is going to take more miles than your tyre will last you need to be confident of being able to replace it en route.

Inner tubes

The greatest danger to inner tubes comes not from punctures but from heat building up as a result of under-inflation. In extreme conditions this can create enough heat to degrade the rubber compound, leading to rapid failure and almost instantaneous deflation. Heavy-duty or super-thick inner tubes can be used in certain circumstances, but they are even more prone to heating up at lower pressures so it is vital that they are kept properly inflated at all times. Keeping a spare inner tube can be a lifesaver, not only for tubed tyres but for tubeless tyres too, in the event of a severe puncture or carcass damage that is too great to be repaired at the roadside.

Fit metal valve caps instead of the more common plastic caps. These can be locked with a spare valve stem locknut, making it hard for little fingers to remove.

Brakes

Overland motorcycling will put huge stress on the motorcycle's braking system. You will be tackling arduous terrain, in hostile and abrasive environments, and your bike will probably be loaded heavily with luggage too. To cope with these conditions the braking system must be in the best possible condition, with fresh pads and fluids as required. If your brake pads are any more than half worn, install new pads simply for the peace of mind they give. Take the old half-worn ones as spares, just in case you need them.

Hydraulic lines also need inspection, especially around flexion points, or areas that can chafe on chassis parts. If there is any indication of cracking, abrasion or any other damage, they will need replacing.

Hydraulic brake fluid also has a limited life and will degrade over time, reducing its efficiency. Changing it is relatively straightforward and should be done every two years, or sooner if there is any significant discoloration or darkening of the fluid.

Control levers need to move smoothly, so be sure to keep the pivots well lubricated with some carefully applied grease. If you have access to any control cables, then take the time to check them for signs of imminent failure such as loose strands of wire or corrosion of the exposed section of cable. Replace them if you have any doubt whatsoever about their integrity. Finally, when all the lubrication tasks have been done, adjust the control cable so the lever has at least 5mm of free movement.

Engine preparation

It goes without saying that your bike's engine must be in tip-top condition for your tour, and the route and duration of your trip will greatly determine what needs to be done. Your owner's manual will have a section listing the items that require attention at various service points and this will give you a good idea of what you will need to do. Unless dealer intervention is required for computer diagnosis, you should be able achieve most tasks without any significant difficulty.

First make a *visual check*. Most fluid or oil leaks are quite obvious, and any discovered will need attending to – leaks rarely get better by themselves, they only ever get worse! Less serious oil leaks will often be revealed by the dirt that is attracted to them, so if your engine casings look dirtier than normal have a look for a leaking rocker or cam-cover gasket.

Check your *oil level*. If it is low then top it up, but if the oil is more than a couple of thousand miles old it is probably best to do a full oil and filter change before you leave, to save having to do it en route. If your oil is new but low then be aware of the rate at which oil is consumed and keep it topped up to maximum level at all times. This is especially important with air-cooled engines as the oil

circuit will very often have a small radiator to assist with supplementary cooling. If you need to top up your oil level regularly be sure to take a small bottle with you just in case you cannot find local supplies.

Remember to check the *coolant systems*. Fluids are often overlooked but can easily be checked. Modern systems are designed to run at pressure and they have an expansion tank that acts as a fluid reservoir. This can usually be easily seen from the side of the motorcycle and the fluid level adjusted accordingly. Check the overall condition of the hoses and replace any that are split or frayed. The coolant fluid will usually need to be changed every two years or so to maintain its effectiveness, so check your owner's manual for the draining and refilling process, being particularly careful to follow any instructions for bleeding air out of the system. When you are refilling, be sure to use a fluid suitable for your engine and check that it is, at the very least, 'silicate free', otherwise you risk ruining water pump seals. The engine should be thoroughly flushed with de-ionised or de-mineralised water to ensure that no old coolant is left behind. The fresh coolant should ideally be a pre-mixed product, or diluted from concentrated anti-freeze with distilled or de-ionised water in a 50/50 mix. Plain tap water should be avoided as its natural mineral content can

↑ **Older technologies do have their advantages!**
📷 Author

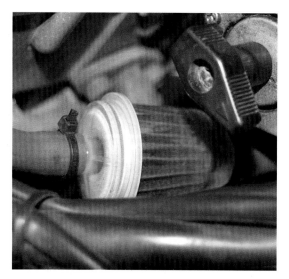

→ A fuel filter is
a cheap but
effective
component for
places where fuel
quality is
uncertain.
📷 Author

Fuel systems and carburation

Modern fuel injection systems are reasonably flexible in respect of dealing with the lower-grade fuels that are often found when touring in more remote areas. Check with your owner's manual to determine how best to approach the problem of low-octane fuels. Some bikes have owner-programmable fuel options, while others will need the fuelling map altered by an authorised dealer.

One of the greatest dangers of 'bush' fuel is the way in which it is stored and handled can easily mean it becomes contaminated with dirt, or it may be older than you think. An in-line fuel filter is a cheap but vital addition to your motorcycle's fuel-delivery circuit and will ensure that no foreign bodies can be carried into the fuel system. A simple car-type filter has a large filter area, is easy to install and easy to flush if it becomes contaminated.

Electrical systems

ADV bikes will generally have an auxiliary power socket fitted somewhere as part of the standard or optional equipment, but there will be many times when you will require another power supply for electrical accessories such as GPS, intercom or additional lighting. To install a power supply to these additional items will require tapping into the bike's wiring loom at some point, or fitting a bespoke fused supply box. Clearly, great care needs to be taken if working with the bike's electrical system as a wrongly connected wire can cause a lot of problems, especially if your machine has a CAN-bus based wiring system.

have adverse effects inside an engine and be responsible for high levels of scaling, especially in hotter parts. Red or pink coolant is often sold as an 'advanced' formula, and it does have some benefits. Having a lower concentration of reactants, it is generally better for an alloy engine, and it has a higher boiling point so it will create less pressure in the cooling system, reducing the risk of splitting a hose.

Unless you are close to a major service date, a 'general' service – one that can be achieved without specialist equipment – will usually be all that is needed to prepare your bike for a tour.

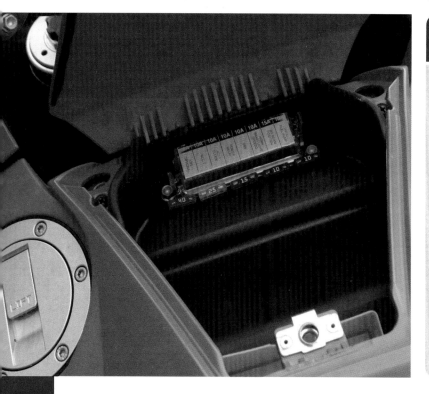

WHAT IS CAN-bus?

In a nutshell, **CAN-bus** – or, to give it the correct name, **controller area network bus** – is a computer-controlled power-distribution system, where each component or circuit is monitored by a specific module within the main computer. Each module can recognise the component and its condition, and will identify any anomalies in its status. As an example, if a bulb fails, it recognises that no current is flowing and will report to the main computer which then flashes an alert on the dashboard display. The **CAN-bus** also determines and controls how much current can supply any individual module, so if it detects too much current flowing in one particular circuit, then the **CAN-bus** will close that circuit down, effectively replacing the need for conventional fuses.

Fitting an additional power outlet need not be that problematic if you have a clear idea of what you need it to do. First, decide what type of supply is needed, and what accessories are likely to be driven by it. If you have high-current equipment such as heated clothing or a small 12v compressor, you will probably need an outlet that is connected directly to the battery. For other accessories, such as GPS or communications equipment, a switched power source will be required.

Second, work out what the current loading is likely to be, and what rating of cable you will need to safely accommodate the demand: 2mm automotive cable has a power rating of 17 amps, which equates to a power loading of 204 watts.

Third, is the outlet going to be 'hot' (permanently live) or switched by the ignition, and what configuration will it be? There are two main types of outlets, the 'cigar lighter' and the 'Hella' type, both of which use different styles of plug. Lower current accessories can be supplied with smaller plugs such as the 2.5mm DC Power Jack, which, when panel-mounted, gives a convenient and low-profile power outlet.

In every case, new or additional circuits need to be protected by an appropriately rated fuse. If you are taking a supply direct from the battery, then the protection fuse must be as close to the battery as possible to minimise the length of 'live' wire in the event of the fuse blowing. If you are installing a fuse block or distribution box, then the main supply cable must be rated and fused according to the total potential load, with individual fuses rated to protect the newly established circuits.

Battery

One other extremely common electrical problem often encountered is having a simple flat battery. Lead/acid, and to a lesser degree maintenance-free batteries, will lose charge over a period of time. This is known as self-discharge, and the rate at which it occurs is usually proportionate to the battery's quality. Self-discharge can occur at any time the battery is in an idle or dormant state, and will usually occur at between 3% and 10% of the battery's capacity in an average month. This figure will be dramatically increased if you have a live alarm or immobiliser fitted to the bike as this makes a constant current demand on the battery. However, the battery can be maintained in peak condition with the use of a battery optimiser which, if used correctly, will constantly monitor the state of the battery and will keep it at an optimum charge level. The clear advantage here is that the bike will always be ready for use, and, if you do have an alarm fitted, it will be kept permanently active.

Voltage meter

It is very easy to assume that the motorcycle will be able to provide power for a lot of accessories, but it is also very easy to underestimate the amount of current you can use. Most

bikes will have an alternator output of around 400 watts, and it does not take much to use almost all of that.

Typical power requirements:

- ■ Ignition & CPU @ 150w = 15A
- ■ Day light @ 55w = 5A
- ■ Auxiliary lights @ 2x55w = 10A
- ■ Heated grips @ 35w = 3A
- ■ Heated gloves @ 25w = 2A
- ■ Heated jacket @ 80w = 7A
- ■ GPS @ 10w = 1A

↑ **An accessory socket is an easy and low-cost upgrade if your bike does not come with one as standard. Fitting it yourself means you can choose where to locate it.**
📷 Lee Parsons

← **A voltage meter is a really useful tool when solving electrical problems. It is also helpful for checking the integrity of any new wiring you have added for accessories.**
📷 Haynes

→ **The effect of corrosion can be catastrophic...**
📷 Author

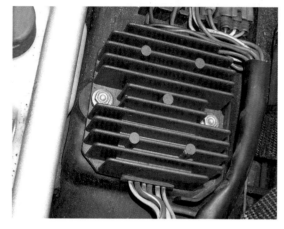

→ **...and it can lead to overheating.**
📷 Haynes

↓ **Replacement with an uprated voltage rectifier/ regulator is the only answer.**
📷 F650FAQ.com

Unfortunately, if you use more power than the alternator can supply, the shortfall will be provided by the reserve held in the battery. For short periods of time this is acceptable and is exactly what the system is supposed to do, but the battery can only store a certain amount of electricity and once that is used up it will be flat. To prevent this situation arising, a very useful accessory is a voltage meter, which allows you to keep an eye on the state of charge of the battery. These are available in various forms, from an in-built digital display of the actual battery voltage, to a simple three-stage LED showing charge, static or drain conditions. With a meter like this you can keep a close check on the state of the battery's charge, and have a good visual indication of the impact that various accessories have on the electrical system. This gives you the option to prioritise your accessory usage while maintaining a healthy charge in the battery.

Voltage rectifier/regulator

The voltage rectifier/regulator (VRR) is a critical component on the bike. Its combined purpose is to convert the AC (alternating current) voltage produced by the alternator into DC (direct current) voltage. It then takes the rectified DC voltage and limits it to a range between 12 and 14 volts, which will be used to charge the battery and supply power to the electrical components of the bike. The energy of the excess voltage is dissipated as heat; however, the components within the VRR are particularly sensitive to overheating, and can fail unpredictably if this happens.

Unfortunately an additional source of heat can come from the high resistance values of poor or corroded connections from the alternator, and all too often this increase in temperature can be too much for the VRR to tolerate. The first sign of a failed VRR will be a boiled battery, the consequences of which are detailed on pages 38–39, but by the time this happens the damage has long been done. The only real solution is to replace the original equipment VRR with an uprated item before your trip. Look for a MOSFET (metal oxide semiconductor field effect transistor) VRR rather than the more common SCR (silicon-controlled rectifier) as this tends to have a higher current capacity and can therefore withstand greater levels of heat. You may have to do some research to discover which VRR can replace yours, and it may not necessarily be from the same brand of motorcycle. If you are confident that your existing VRR is good, the possibility of high-resistance problems can be greatly reduced by removing the blade connector altogether and soldering the joints together.

Damage limitation

Taking a tumble will be almost inevitable during a tour, and even a simple slow-speed tip-over can cause damage to your motorcycle that is both costly and potentially

tour-breaking. Various accessories can be fitted which will minimise this risk.

Most vulnerable are the handlebar control levers which, despite having a designed-in fracture point, will often break in the wrong place or bend, rendering them useless. In the worst case a tumble could break either the lever pivot or the handlebar clamp, both of which will be very difficult, even impossible, to repair. Levers can be protected by leaving the clamp slightly loose, which will allow a degree of rotation on the handlebar that will very often be enough to save the lever. Using a couple of turns of PTFE plumbing tape under the clamp also allows you to tighten it enough to prevent loosening while still letting it turn on the bar in the event of an impact. Fitting hinged levers is another ingenious, if slightly expensive, solution.

Both foot pedals can be protected with a 'snake', which is simply a steel cable attached to the tip of the pedal and a forward point on the bike to limit how far the pedal will move or be bent in an impact. A 'snake' can also prevent scrub or low-lying branches getting caught between the lever and the crankcase.

An original-equipment mirror is usually extremely expensive to replace, more so if it is clamped to the handlebar as part of a control lever assembly, with the risk of the clamp being broken too. Using a ball-clamp-mounted mirror is a cheap and very effective solution, especially as each part can be purchased separately.

Protection systems

Under the broad heading of accessories come items designed to protect various components. You must decide, of course, which you think are necessities, as some have genuinely useful functions while others are simply adornments of little more than cosmetic value. Generally speaking, the components that are most exposed particularly need protection: a specific example is the headlamp, which can be protected from stones either by a polycarbonate cover or a wire-mesh screen.

Arguably one of the most vulnerable areas of the bike is its underside, with the sump plate and exhaust pipes/ CAT system, and very often the oil filter too, exposed to stones thrown up by the front wheel. Most ADV bikes will have a bash-plate fitted, but often it will only offer minimal protection. After-market sump guards are available for most models and will shield virtually the whole of the underside of the bike, protecting those exposed components as well as giving you a useful skid-plate.

Engine bars or crash bars create a protective cage

↑ **Protection systems will often save broken body panels.**
📷 Thorvaldur Orn Kristmundsson

➜ The side-mounted tanks of a KTM 950/990 can be vulnerable.
📷 KTM UK Ltd.

➜ Mudguard extensions are a great addition if your travels involve lots of tarmac, but clearance can be limited if you have fitted off-road rubber.
📷 Lee Parsons

around the engine, safeguarding the motorcycle if it falls on to its side, especially if you have a bike with low-slung or side-mounted tanks. If fitted in conjunction with hand guards they can very often provide virtually complete side protection, keeping the fragile engine casings off the ground in the event of a spill.

The bike's radiators for both oil and engine cooling are critical components that are rarely protected as well as they should be. On a liquid-cooled machine the radiator will usually be in a vulnerable position, especially in off-road situations where it is directly in the line of

fire from any stones or pebbles that could be thrown up by the front wheel. If left without adequate protection there is a good chance that sooner or later it will suffer damage as a result. Your bike will probably have some basic plastic protection as fitted ex-factory, but a sturdy metal item will offer a significant degree of extra protection. A second line of defence can be obtained by fitting a mudguard extension or 'fender extender'. These extenders work very well on tarmac by keeping road spray and debris out of the fins of the radiator, but they can compromise off-road ability.

➜ Bike-specific radiator guards are available from many different manufacturers. Most fit quickly and easily using existing radiator mountings.
📷 Author

Accessories

There are literally hundreds of accessories available for almost every ADV bike ever built. From auxiliary lighting systems to brake pedal extension pieces, full luggage packs to a small strap-on bag, the list can sometimes seem endless and certainly too extensive to discuss fully here. However, there are a few 'essentials' to consider.

Global positioning system, more commonly known as GPS, is one family of accessories that has gained tremendous popularity in recent years, and what once used to be considered high-end navigation systems are now in very common use. Thankfully, as technology has advanced, they have become smaller to handle, cheaper to buy and much easier to use, making them a much more attractive proposition for use on a motorcycle. These units need to be securely mounted, not only from the point of view of road travel, but also to prevent light fingers spiriting them away while you are not looking. Modern units are small and light and can safely be mounted on the handlebars without fear of upsetting the handling or getting in the way of the controls. There will be two parts to most GPS mounts: the first will be specific to the model of GPS receiver you are using; the second will attach it to the bodywork or handlebars of the bike. Installing one is relatively simple as long as you have access to a power supply, or can break into the bike's loom at a convenient point.

If your bike is chain-driven, a very sensible addition would be an automatic chain-lubricating system. There will be a model-specific fitment available for most bikes, but a

'universal' kit will do the job just as well. Fitting one can be a little fiddly, as it will involve finding a suitable mounting location for the oil-delivery meter, and a remote reservoir if fitted. Many of these systems rely upon low pressure in the inlet tract to control the oil flow, so you also have to be able to access the motor and carburation or injection system, which will generally involve removing the petrol tank or air filter box. Once fitted, however, the headache of having to manually lubricate the drive chain disappears, with several thousand miles being possible before the lubricant needs to be replenished. Once adjusted properly

↑ **This extended screen shields both the rider and his accessories!**
📷 Lee Parsons

← **An automatic chain oiler will extend a chain's useful life.**
📷 Author

modification it is vital that the power supply is adequately fused to protect the rest of the bike.

When mounting the lights always make sure that they can be securely fixed, and that the mounting point will be strong and rigid enough to support the lights. Check that the fork legs or any control cables do not foul or touch the mounting in any way.

Always consider the extra electrical demand that accessories like auxiliary lights will place on the alternator, and make sure that you always have sufficient charging current available to keep the bike's battery healthy.

Luggage

Luggage will always be a contentious matter, especially as both styles of luggage – either hard box systems or soft panniers – have their advantages. Hard luggage can be bulky and often heavy, but it offers high levels of protection not only to your stuff but to the bike as well in the case of a spill. Aluminium cases can distort on impact, however, and can be hard to straighten back into a watertight and secure unit. Soft luggage is light and extremely portable, but it is not particularly immune from either theft or impact. If soft panniers get damaged, however, they can be repaired with a variety of materials to restore their functionality. Both systems will need some kind of sub-frame to be fitted to the chassis: hard cases require their own mounting system and soft luggage needs some additional means of preventing contact with either the exhaust or the rear wheel. Other options are mounting small bags on the engine bars, or tank-mounted soft panniers.

↑ Auxiliary lights can be fitted with high-intensity discharge (HID) systems for ultimate performance.
📷 Rugged Roads Ltd.

there is little mess, and chain life can be extended by a factor of two or three.

Unless you are exceptionally lucky and have excellent lights fitted as standard, you will probably be thinking about supplementing your bike's lighting. What system you fit will depend largely upon the effect you hope to achieve – visibility or 'presence' requires a bright but broad spread of light, while improved night vision requires a narrower, more directed beam pattern. Assuming you have a suitable mounting point, fitting either system will be very similar, whichever you decide upon. As with any electrical

➜ Semi-rigid luggage can often provide the most flexible solution.
📷 Famsa

Travelling toolkit

There is no definitive 'best toolkit', or even an ideal toolkit. In fact the only toolkit you will ever be really interested in is the one you are carrying when you need it – what goes into it is up to you!

Part of the joy of ADV motorcycling is the thrill of the unknown, the challenge attached to problem-solving and the risk attached to what you are doing. How does a toolkit fit into all of this? Simple – it is the one element of your travelling kit that enables you to solve problems and overcome mechanical obstacles. With a little thought you can create a toolkit that is comprehensive enough to deal with most problems you are likely to face, yet small and compact enough to carry and stow easily.

Different types of tools will be required owing to the nature of the travelling you are planning and the damage that you are likely to incur. The first mistake that almost everyone makes, however, is to take too much stuff: we have all done it and we have probably all taken tools that never saw the light of day on our journeys! If you follow a few basic rules you can build a toolkit that will get you out of most of the trouble you are likely to encounter.

Rule 1: Don't take what you don't need!

It is all too easy to tell yourself you are taking something 'just in case', but you will simply end up taking too many things. Look at your bike, look at your tools. The socket set you have bought for the trip has a nice case to keep everything tidy, but do you really need an 11mm socket? By looking at your bike and checking the fasteners it uses you can see what tools you might need, and you can leave the tools behind that will not fit anything!

Rule 2: Keep it small, keep it light!

There are very few fasteners on a motorcycle that need high torque values to fasten them properly. Check in your manual for the various torque settings for an idea of the numbers involved. The two biggest that spring to mind are perhaps the rear wheel axle nut and the clutch basket nut. You have a lovely ½-inch drive socket set at home, capable of handling more torque than you can apply, but it will be bulky and it will be heavy. A good-quality ⅜-inch drive wrench will be able to handle almost as much torque as a ½-inch drive, and certainly as much as most motorcycle applications will need. For example, the Teng ⅜th driver featured in the toolkit can handle more than twice as much torque as the 100Nm that is required to fasten the rear axle nut on most motorcycles, although in extreme circumstances you might need to use an extension tube on the handle to get the extra leverage required.

Rule 3: Make a tool do more than one job

Use a socket drive adaptor to allow you to use ½-inch sockets with a ⅜th wrench. Some tools are purpose-designed to serve two functions, an ideal example of this being the combo tyre lever – a high-strength 7075 T6 aluminium alloy lever with a tyre spoon on one end and a hex wrench on the other. Various wrench sizes are available – an ideal combination is the rear axle nut size – and attachments can be used to transform it into a socket driver too.

The other obligatory tool to carry must be a multi-tool such as a Leatherman or Gerber. These pack a huge variety of tools into one very compact package. The Leatherman Surge, for example, has some 22 tool functions which can be further extended by the addition of various adaptors. Quality has to be an issue to consider here, as these tools will give a lifetime's service if looked after and used properly.

Rule 4: Evaluate the risk, then prioritise your toolkit accordingly

If you know your bike well enough, then you will also have an idea of its potential weaknesses or areas of high maintenance need. Being aware of these factors also helps in the decision-making process for taking the appropriate tools – for example, if you know you will be riding a lot of miles on rough surfaces or other rocky terrain, a puncture repair kit is essential. Some bikes have known weaknesses: immobilisation antennas or wheel bearings for example. If you know there is a higher-than-average chance of a problem, be sure to take appropriate spares and the tools needed to fit them.

⬇ **Pack only the tools you will really need.**
📷 Andreas Hülsmann

THE ESSENTIAL TOOL KIT

Electrical
- Insulating tape or self-amalgamating tape
- Scotch locks
- Small screwdriver
- Spare fuses and cable
- Bulb set
- Battery or gas powered soldering iron + solder

Pneumatic
- **Puncture repair kit** (check it is compatible with your tyre/tube)
- Spare valve cores and caps
- Tyre irons or levers – 2 x 12 inch + 1 x 7 inch
- Spanners/wrenches for wheel axles
- Small 12v compressor or mini bicycle pump
- Tyre pressure gauge

Mechanical
- **Wrenches/sockets to fit fasteners**
  Ratcheting spanners are very useful in confined spaces and can deliver almost as much torque as a socket driver.
- Stubby spanners – again to fit fasteners
- Screwdrivers – Phillips and conventional
- Allen or Torx keys
- Small pliers/molegrips
- Circlip pliers
- Magnetic pick-up tool
- Chain tool and spare links/spring clips
- Leatherman multi-tool
- Stubby-handled hammer
- Short length of steel drift/through screwdriver
- Spoke wrench

Miscellaneous
- **Plastic sheet or tarpaulin**
  Essential to lay out under the bike if you are working on earth or sand where you could easily drop and lose small components.
- **Rubber or latex gloves**
  Great to use in areas where you can't easily clean your hands after a dirty procedure; they keep the inside of your riding gloves clean, too.
- **Condoms**
  Useful for keeping matches dry and can also be used as an emergency water carrier.
- A length of steel Bowden cable and a selection of screw nipples
- Epoxy adhesive or 'chemical metal'
- Hose clips or 'Jubilee' clips
- Coolant hose repair tape
- Self-tapping screw selection
- Small selection of appropriate fasteners
- Gaffer tape or duct tape
- WD40 or similar dry-film aerosol lubricant

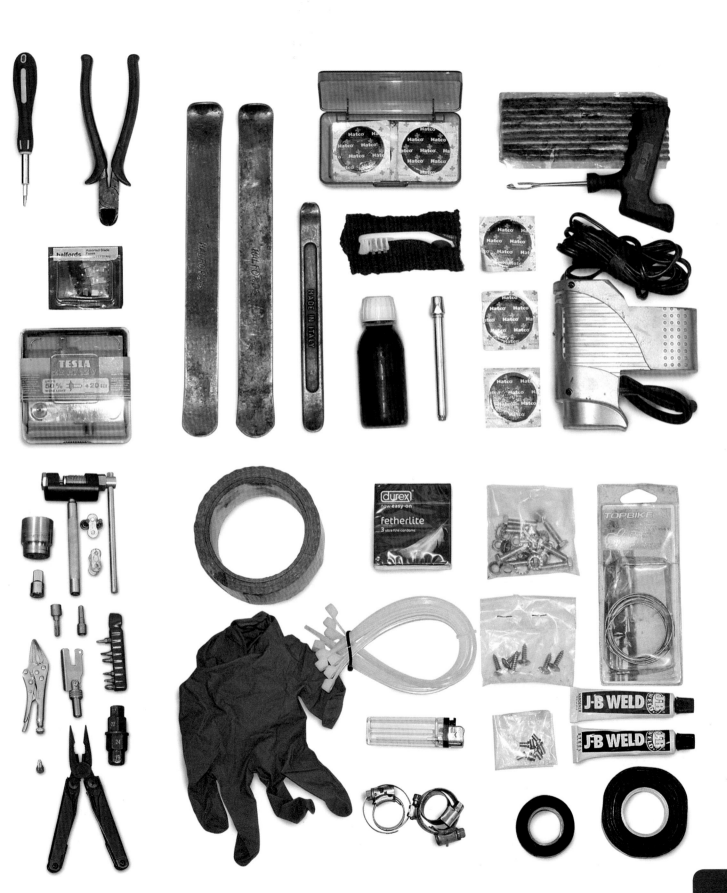

Diagnostic tools

CAN-bus has been mentioned briefly in various parts of this book and, like it or not, this is a growing technology and is to be found in all high-end ADV bikes currently available. While this technology brings a flexibility and sophistication beyond the capacity of conventional hard-wired electrical control systems, it also means that fault-finding is a lot more difficult as the computer-controlled 'brain' will more often than not simply shut the whole bike down.

The computerised control systems found on many modern cars and motorcycles these days are extremely complex and require sophisticated equipment to use them effectively. Using a full diagnostic computer is a skilful task, requiring not only the hardware but also the software needed to read and interpret the fault codes, and ultimately reset the system or component to function within its required parameters. The complexity of these systems is advancing constantly, with the most current systems being able to download bike-specific data on to a central database. This degree of connectivity allows vast amounts of information to be stored and will let any networked dealer access the bike's history, identifying all service operations and upgrade or recall work conducted.

Thankfully, a simplified device for reading the fault codes stored in the bike's memory is available at a fraction of the cost. Known as a 'code reader', it allows the user to interrogate the diagnostic system to see what fault codes have been flagged and which system has been compromised by any failed component. Model-specific readers will

also display real-time data, and allow certain components and systems to be tested in isolation, as well as identifying any anomalous readings which might generally indicate an imminent failure. Their real benefit will come if ever a component fails while travelling, and using one to interrogate the system will allow the user to identify the problem rapidly and, if necessary, make arrangements for replacement components to be ordered and shipped.

Most Japanese motorcycles can display fault codes on their dashboard if a 'service plug' is connected to the diagnostic socket. The same result can very often also be achieved by 'jumping' specific terminals of the diagnostic socket with a wire link, although you must be sure that you know which terminals to connect. The resulting codes can be shown as a number in the display panel, or occasionally a sequence of warning light flashes. Interpreting these codes can sometimes be difficult, but a little web-based research will usually reveal the answer.

Spares

There will always be a few key items that will be essential to pack, although it will always be difficult to predict what you'll need! Try to keep whatever you take to a minimum, certainly only taking those items that you know might or will be difficult to source in the area where you will be travelling, but remember that smaller items such as spare brake pads and wheel bearings take up no room at all in your luggage. Research your route, identifying points on the way where you can access garage services or dealer facilities. Check with the various owners' groups to research your bike's weak points

and use that knowledge as part of the preparation process to replace items that have a history of failure, or those which will wear out before your return. Thankfully catastrophic mechanical failures are relatively rare these days, especially if you are diligent with your service schedules, but smaller items such as control cables are always at risk. Buy replacements for your key cables, and fit them before you leave, but leave the 'old' ones in situ. That way you know for sure that the spare works (because you've already fitted it) and you also have a guaranteed suitable replacement already in place (the 'old' one) in the event of the new ones failing.

Spare bulbs for your main lights are essential, and are a legal requirement in some countries. Keep a set in your electrical toolkit, along with a selection of fuses.

One of the most vital spares to take is a duplicate ignition key. Surprisingly, many motorcycle travellers leave home with just one key, but in this day and age of hyper-sophisticated alarms and immobilisers, if you lose yours it is very unlikely that you'll ever get the bike running without it. There are suitable hidey-holes on every bike that can be used to stow a spare key – you just need to remember where you put it! When securing a spare, make sure it's not going to become dislodged, or fall out easily. Don't chose an obvious place like under the seat, or behind the number plate, or secure it to

SELF-PRESERVATION

There will always be the rare occasion when you break down and are unable to make any progress at all. In these situations NEVER LEAVE YOUR MOTORCYCLE. You and it are far more visible together. While it might seem that you are in the middle of a wilderness, the reality is that you are quite likely to see someone coming along the road before too long. Don't be afraid to be assertive when trying to get them to stop, although once they see your plight most fellow travellers will be more than happy to help. Hitch a ride to the nearest town, and you'll probably find that your travelling friend will help you here too, in seeking recovery and repair of the bike. Most mechanics in remote areas have learned how to keep almost any vehicle running and they might well be able to offer a solution. At worst you'll be able to find a phone and call home for spares to be freighted to you.

anything that might become detached from the bike, like a rear mudguard, for example. Ideally, it should be in its own small waterproof container, one that can be either zip-tied or fixed to the bike's bodywork.

One of the most appealing aspects of motorcycling is the chance for the rider to express themselves through their bike. From the sports bike that almost demands the rider to wear garish leathers to street cruisers that are built for show and not comfort, every bike allows the rider to make their own statement. Adventure motorcycles are no exception to this, but in the main the majority of accessories and modifications actually do make functional and useful enhancements to the motorcycle and its abilities.

There is no single bike that is 'journey ready' as soon as it is ridden out of the showroom, but the list of potential modifications that can be made to a modern ADV bike is almost endless – you only have to look in any of the accessory manufacturers' catalogues to see pages and pages of equipment that can be attached to your motorcycle. A large part of the enjoyment of owning an ADV bike comes from being able to 'tailor' the bike to suit your exact requirements, to make it as individual as you are. There is no doubt that some extras are quite functional, some even essential, but a lot may simply be expensive trinkets and gadgets that do no more than offer a distraction.

While it might initially seem daunting, especially if you have never attempted this kind of work before, most of the jobs you are likely to do will be more than achievable with a little forethought and preparation. As long as you take your time and approach the tasks systematically and methodically, success will be waiting for you just round the next corner!

As with any task you perform on the bike, take the time to become familiar with what you want to do, read any instructions that come with the kit, and make sure you have all the tools required to do the job. Having to stop the job halfway through to go and buy a missing tool is frustrating enough, but completely ruining the project by using the wrong tool is ten times worse and twice as expensive!

Electrical projects can sometimes represent quite a challenge in keeping things tidy; indeed carelessly installed wiring will always give you a problem sooner or later. Rather than struggle trying to thread wiring through small gaps and spaces, it can be more effective to spend a few minutes removing a couple of body panels to see how the wiring can best be routed. Doing this will keep the supplementary cables out of danger and will also let you secure them to other parts of the wiring harness. Take care to identify the locations of each fastener as you will find that some may have different sizes and threads.

Great care must be taken with any electrical modification – even a single pair of lights can put quite a high loading on the bike's electrical system. Check your bike's alternator output – it should be given in the owner's manual – and make sure it has enough output to power your accessories *and* keep the battery charged (see page 37). Also check the power rating (wattage) of the accessory you are fitting and be sure to use the right cable – a pair of 55w lights will consume around 10A, requiring a minimum of 2mm^2 cable – and fit an appropriately rated in-line fuse to protect the wiring you are about to install.

Fitting most accessories will take a bit of thought, but with a little preparation almost anyone can achieve a great result and feel the satisfaction of being able to stand back and say: 'I did that!'

PROTECTION & RIDER COMFORT

One of the pivotal requirements of an adventure motorcycle is the ability to cover significant distances if required to do so. The reality, however, is that any motorcycle can cover huge distances, but the limiting factor is how long the rider can comfortably stay in the saddle. Imagine a position similar to sitting on an average dining chair with your forearms resting on the table in front of you – within a few degrees you have a perfect overlanding riding position. The bike's handlebars should encourage you to lean slightly forward – not too far though or you will risk lower back pain. If they are too high then you will have an aching neck and shoulders in no time. Likewise footrests should have a neutral position, in much the same place as your feet would be while sitting on that dining chair.

Changing the screen for an aftermarket option offering increased wind protection will reduce the physical strain of day-long riding, as will the fitting of hand guards. Remember, removing the distraction of discomfort increases the level of concentration you can apply to your riding, keeping you more alert and safer in the long run.

Hand guards, bash plates and the other forms of motorcycle protection also serve to provide peace of mind in the event of dropping the bike, ensuring that the journey will be able to proceed regardless of terrain or road conditions.

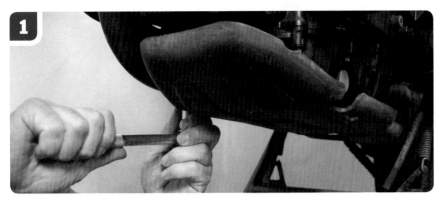

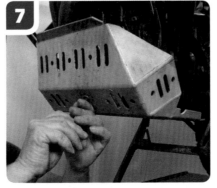

The standard-equipment bash plate fitted to most ADV bikes is usually quite minimalist and gives very limited protection to the vulnerable underside of the engine. An aftermarket bash plate will be manufactured using high-grade materials and will be capable of withstanding the rigours of overlanding while protecting the bike's underbelly. Metal Mule's plate for the BMW F800GS is constructed using 4mm thick NS4 grade aluminium plate, and has a wrap-around design which protects not only the sump but also the engine's side casings as well as the otherwise exposed oil filter cartridge and front-mounted oil cooler. It is an essential modification for serious overlanding.

1. Remove the original-equipment sump protector. Be aware that some plates will have flexible rubber mounts to give enough movement to simplify oil filter changes, and will have fasteners with a secondary bolt head underneath the plate.
2. Fit any supplementary brackets required. This Metal Mule shield is quite long to give protection to the oil filter and requires an extended mounting bracket.
3. Ensure that the bracket is correctly aligned and oriented.
4. Offer up the plate to the mounting points.
5. Engage the plate on the rearmost rubber mounting.
6. Tighten the rear rubber mounting positions...
7. ...before making the final attachment with the front mounting points, ensuring all fasteners are securely tightened.

Rough and stony terrain can prove a challenge for any accessory on an adventure motorcycle, none more so than the headlight. Just one pebble thrown up by the bike in front can break or crack the lens, after which the only repair possible is a very expensive replacement. A guard in front of the lens is a simple fitment and a cost-effective investment.

Headlight guards tend to be model-specific and usually take the form of a mesh or machined metal grille that fixes in front of the original light on additional brackets, like the one illustrated here, but clear plastic covers that fix directly to the original headlight glass are also available. For off-road riding, particularly on gravel tracks, a metal guard offers increased levels of protection against larger pieces of debris.

Most guards are specified for daytime use only and should be removed if riding at night – you have been told!

1   Loosen the bolts securing the headlight housing to the mounting frame.
2   Remove the bolts, taking care not to let the headlight unit fall. Offer up the protector to the mounting frame.
3   Check clearances around supplied brackets, paying particular attention to any wiring.
4   Replace the mounting bolts.
5   Make a final visual check that everything is in place. Readjust the headlight alignment if necessary.

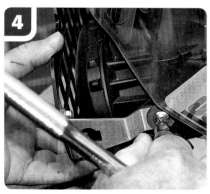

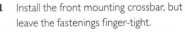

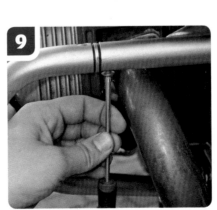

Apart from oil starvation, most damage to engines is caused by crashing the bike or it falling over. Fitting engine-protection bars will prevent or minimise this risk, especially in the case of the exposed cylinders of a BMW boxer twin.

1   Install the front mounting crossbar, but leave the fastenings finger-tight.
2   Attach the lower mounting brackets, ensuring correct alignment.
3   Offer up the first side bar locating the lug in the lower bracket, and the upper tube in the front crossbar.
4   Insert the front crossbar retaining screw.
5   Loosely secure the lower mounting lug.
6   Offer up the other side bar, again locating the lower lug and upper tube mounting. Insert the remaining crossbar retaining screw.
7   Tighten the lower mounting lugs to the recommended torque figure.
8   Tighten the front mounting crossbar fasteners to the recommended torque figure.
9   Tighten both crossbar retaining screws.
10 Stand back and admire your work!

Most liquid-cooled motorcycles place the radiator in front of the engine for maximum airflow. Unfortunately this position makes the radiator vulnerable to damage from stones and other debris flicked up by the front wheel or passing vehicles. A metal guard placed in front of the radiator will offer increased protection against impact damage.

1 Radiator guards are bike-specific so ensure you purchase the correct one for your model of bike.

2 Most guards are easy to fit and rely on the existing radiator mounting points for support. Consider fitting some foam-rubber strips to the back of the guard – this will help cushion the fitting between guard and radiator and will help with the airflow around the guard.

3 Take the opportunity to give the radiator a thorough clean before you proceed with the fitting as it will be difficult to do so once the guard is in place.

4 Remove the existing mounting bolts, taking care not to dislodge the radiator or the fan. You should be able to fit the guard without removing the radiator.

5 Some guards utilise the original fitting hardware, some supply replacements. Often a combination of the two can provide the best solution overall. Make sure you retain any old or unused fittings in case you need to remove the guard later.

6 Offer up the guard and check the fit. On some motorcycles you may wish to modify the fittings in order to improve airflow. On this bike it was preferable to add a few washers between the bracket on the guard and the radiator mountings in order to relieve the strain placed on the brackets.

7 Once you are happy with the fit, tighten down the fastenings and check that the radiator is securely in position.

8 Re-check fittings after riding the bike, and pay close attention to the running temperature once the guard is in place.

Not all adventure bikes leave the factory with hand protection fitted as standard. Fortunately there are many aftermarket hand guards available, from simple brush guards to aluminium-spined wrap-around designs offering high levels of impact protection. The design shown here is similar to the ones that KTM fits to its 990 Adventure.

1   Remove any existing bar end weights, if fitted, and check to make sure the fastening kit will fit the end of the bars.
2   Undo any cable ties that might interfere with the fitting of the hand guards.
3   Offer up the guards to check fitting.
4   Install the bar end fitting bolt and expanding wedge in the end of the hand guard.
5   Fit the expanding bolt into the end of the handlebar and loosely tighten.
6   Install the hand guard bar clamp inboard of the levers and tighten just enough to hold in place. Check the clearance and operation of the brake lever, clutch lever and throttle, making sure the hand guards do not impede movement. Levers can be moved inboard a little to provide clearance, and if required trim the end of the throttle tube to ensure smooth operation.
7   Rotate steering through full left and right travel, checking cables and hand guards for clearance with bodywork and screen. Tighten all fastenings to specified torque.
8   Reinstall cable ties, paying particular attention to revised cable runs.
9   If your motorcycle suffers from excessive vibration through the bars, check to see if you can utilise the original bar weights to secure the end of the hand guards – some hand guards come with replacement weights in the fitting kit.

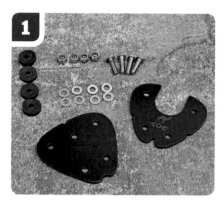

Any motorcycle with off-road pretentions should be able to stand up on a soft surface, yet most leave the factory with side-stand feet so small that they sink easily into soft ground, especially if the motorcycle is laiden with luggage.

Fitting a side-stand base extension should be considered essential in your tour preparation – fortunately it is not difficult.

Depending on the make and model of your motorcycle you will find a wide variety of designs available – they all do the same job and most attach in the same way.

You could just weld a larger plate of steel to the bottom of the existing foot, but aftermarket plates are easier to remove when you come to sell up and can be replaced more easily if they become damaged.

1 Check the kit contains everything needed for your motorcycle.
2 Place the motorcycle on its centre stand, or have a friend hold it upright to raise the side stand from the floor.
3 Offer up the top plate and bottom plate to ensure it will fit – irregular welding at the base of the side stand can occasionally make fitting tricky and might require you to file off a little of the top plate to ensure a good fit.
4 Lightly grease and attach the bolts and rubber spacers to the bottom plate.
5 Offer up the plate to the side-stand foot – you may need to trim a little off the rubber spacers to ensure a good fit. Consider applying a little grease to the existing side-stand foot as it will be difficult to clean once the two plates are tightened in place and corrosion might develop where existing paint has worn away.
6 Fit the top plate and use washers and thread-locking nuts to secure in place – if nylon thread-locking nuts are not available, consider using some thread-lock compound to help secure the nuts.
7 Tighten the fitting hardware to securely clamp the two plates on to the side-stand foot. Check that it is secure and cannot be dislodged. Fold up the side stand as for riding and check clearance with the swing arm and centre stand (if fitted).
8 Lean the motorcycle carefully back on to the side stand and check that the base extension sits flush with the floor.

The area around the rear wheel of your motorcycle is quite hostile – stones and road debris can be picked up and thrown by the tread in the tyre, while water spray and mud can coat the suspension unit with the risk of damage to the seal and damper rod. A hugger is designed to prevent this happening and will shield the underside of the bike from the worst of the contamination.

1 Remove the existing chain guard, and keep the fixings to hand.
2 Displace brake lines and ABS sensor cables if required.
3 Offer up the hugger, ensuring that all drillings line up with the mounting holes.
4 Install the fixings, ensuring that they are not overtightened.
5 Check that the wheel rotates freely and that the hugger does not foul the chassis.

Fitting an oiling system for your drive chain is a reasonably simple task that requires only a few tools, and it can be completed in a couple of hours. When properly installed, the oiler will clean and protect your transmission, and will make a great difference to the lifetime of the chain and sprockets.

There are a variety of systems available but most employ the same basic principle of using gravity to deliver lubricating oil to the drive chain, with the flow rate controlled either by vacuum or an electronic switch known as a remote metering valve (RMV). Whichever system you choose, the basic fitting operation will be the same, requiring a mounting point for the oil reservoir, and either a switched power supply or a source of vacuum to control the oil flow.

Take the time to read the instructions properly and check the manufacturer's website for any bike-specific considerations that will have to be taken into account. If you are fitting a vacuum-controlled oiler, it is imperative that you use only the recommended vacuum take-off point. This is especially important if your bike is fuel injected, as many injection

systems have air-bleed lines that are designed to have lower pressure, but will drastically upset the bike's fuelling if disturbed. Check also where the oil-delivery nozzle will be located and how it will be secured to the swing arm. The oil must be delivered to the right point of the chain, otherwise it will not do its job of lubricating the chain and its 'O' rings to keep friction to a minimum.

Go through the fitting instructions to familiarise yourself with the various parts of the kit and where they will be fitted to the bike. Do a 'loose fit' first, and do not cut any of the oil or vacuum pipes until you are certain that everything is correct.

1. Offer up the components to the bike, 'loose fitting' with cable ties.
2. Check where you will be routing the various pipes.
3. Remove or displace bodywork where necessary to allow access to vacuum points.
4. Install the vacuum take-off spigot and fit the damper elbow.
5. Connect the main vacuum pipe and feed it to the RMV, avoiding kinks and hot spots.
6. Connect the oil-delivery pipe to the spigot on the bottom of the RMV and route the pipe along the swing arm, fixing it in place with the clips/channel supplied.
7. Fix the adjustable oil-delivery nib holder to a suitable place on the swing arm and bend it to adjust the delivery of oil to the recommended point.
8. Fill the RMV with the supplied oil and set to 'prime' to fill the delivery pipe and nib.
9. Start the engine and set the oil delivery rate as recommended to 1–2 drops per minute.

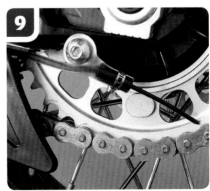

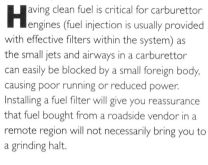

1

Having clean fuel is critical for carburettor engines (fuel injection is usually provided with effective filters within the system) as the small jets and airways in a carburettor can easily be blocked by a small foreign body, causing poor running or reduced power. Installing a fuel filter will give you reassurance that fuel bought from a roadside vendor in a remote region will not necessarily bring you to a grinding halt.

1 Start with as little fuel in the tank as possible. Close the petcock and disconnect the fuel line. Be careful as residual fuel can still flow. Mop up any spillage (see the safety hints on pages 17–18) and ventilate your working space. If you have a large or extended-range fuel tank, it may need to be removed to give access to the fuel lines and carburettor.

2 The fuel filter has a stepped spigot at either end and can be used with different-sized fuel lines. Note the arrow indicating the direction of fuel flow.

3 Select a suitable place to install the fuel filter and push it firmly into the fuel line, remembering that it is directional.

4 Use cable ties to secure the fuel line – screw-type clamps may crush the filter's spigots.

5 Refit the fuel tank if removed, then reconnect the fuel line and open the petcock. If you have fuel seepage the filter may need to be pushed further into the fuel line or the cable ties tightened.

2

3

4

5

Quite often the standard screen will not suit the rider, and fitting an aftermarket replacement will generally give better wind protection for higher-speed riding. This is one of the simplest jobs to do, and makes an excellent start for the novice.

1   Offer up the replacement screen to check mounting points before proceeding.
2   Remove the original screen. Check fasteners – some screens use specialist well-nuts that are captive in the mounting frame.
3   Offer up the new screen, installing the uppermost fixing first, finger-tight. Insert remaining fixings and any nylon washers, again all finger-tight, until all are fitted.
4   Check the alignment of the screen and carefully tighten the fittings. Check that the travel of the handlebars is not compromised by the screen.

Fitting spoilers

Spoilers are small deflectors that are fitted to the bike's bodywork just below the screen. They act as small spoilers and supplement the function of the screen by deflecting airflow around the rider's torso.

1   Use the supplied template on the bodywork to mark/prepare for drilling.
2   Using the correct size of twist drill, make the appropriate mounting holes.
3   Insert the self-securing well nuts.
4   Install the spoilers, being careful not to overtighten the fixings.
5   Check that the travel of the handlebars is not compromised by the screen.

ELECTRICAL ACCESSORIES

he very nature of the ADV bike sets it apart from other mainstream motorcycles. The potential for adding accessories is quite simply huge and much of this extra equipment will require electrical power.

We are all very aware of the risks that lurk in the realms of high-voltage electricity, and the dangers attached to domestic mains voltages have been covered elsewhere in this book. But just because we are dealing with a 'mere' 12V in a typical motorcycle circuit does not mean to say that it is all 'sparks and larks'. In an uncontrolled short circuit, 12V can produce an extremely high current flow which – unless the circuit is protected by a fuse – can generate very high temperatures within the wiring. These temperatures can be high enough to melt the copper core of a cable and certainly melt a cable's insulation, thus exposing the 'live' wire within.

In this section we will take a look at how to fit and install electrical accessories safely, and – most important of all – how to protect the various circuits from overloading and potential failure.

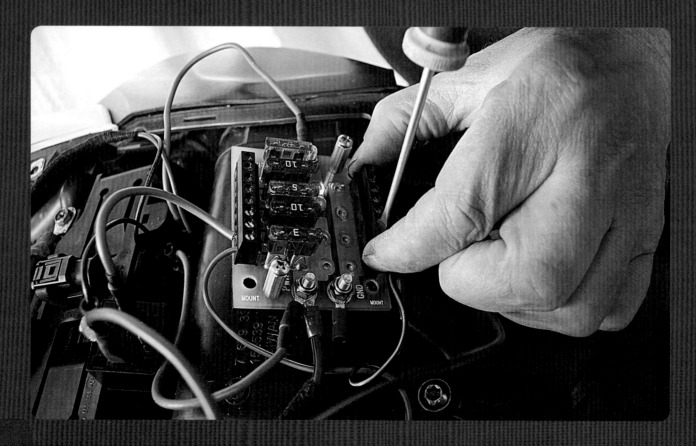

One of the first things that many owners will want to do to their ADV bike is fit some accessories and gadgets. Most of these accessories will require power and it is not always appropriate or possible to attach multiple ring connectors to the positive terminal of the battery to provide the electrical power that each accessory needs. Fitting an auxiliary fuse panel provides the option of multiple power access points, each of which can be appropriately fused according to the demand placed on it by the accessory. Some of the higher-end panels also have two separate power inputs, giving much greater flexibility and allowing some of the fused outputs to be permanently live while others will remain controlled by the ignition switch.

Fitting the auxiliary power panel is likely to require the removal of some body panels, so familiarise yourself with where it is going to be best placed and remove bodywork accordingly. Identify also a convenient and safe route for the main power cable, such that it will not be kinked or compressed anywhere along its length.

The fuse panel will have a maximum current rating (amperage) that must not be exceeded, so be sure that each power outlet is fused appropriately for the accessories that it will supply, and that the total fuse amperage is not greater than the rating of the panel. As with any live voltage feed, insert a master fuse as close to the battery terminal as conveniently accessible, so that if ever the cable does chafe and blow the fuse, the length of cable which remains 'live' will be as short as possible.

Great care must be taken at every stage of this procedure to prevent short circuits, so if possible disconnect the battery to isolate the bike's wiring loom. Check with your manual whether an interruption of power to the ECU will trigger any warnings; for example, some BMW models will show 'SERVICE' in the on-board computer display if the battery has been disconnected. Unless you have your own code-reader, this system alert can only be removed by your dealer. If this is the case, ensure that the supplementary cable's master fuse is removed from the holder.

Materials & tools

- Cable – colour-coded if required
- 12v switching relay
- Master fuse holder
- Wire cutters
- Crimp connectors and crimping tool

1 Identify a suitable location for the fuse panel and a power source.
2 Take a length of twin-core red and black coded cable of a gauge sufficient to handle the maximum potential current – 30A will need a 2mm^2 cable. Always cut your cable a little longer than you think you will need, then cut to the exact length when you make the final installation. Prepare the main feed cable by crimping 6mm ring terminals to one end of the cable. and place the fuse panel in its preferred location.

HOW TO CALCULATE YOUR FUSE RATING

The wattage of the accessory divided by the circuit voltage equals the current it uses. So a 55w auxiliary light supplied by 12v will require a 5A fuse (55÷12=4.58).

Typical current requirements
- Auxiliary lights @ 2x55w=10A
- Heated grips @ 35w=3A
- Heated gloves @ 25w=2A
- Heated jacket @ 80w=7A
- GPS @ 10w=1A

3 Connect the red (+ve) and black (−ve) cables to the panel.

4 Route the cable back to the battery or power source, ensuring it is not trapped or snagged.

5 Install an in-line fuse holder (without the fuse) in the red (+ve) cable as close to the battery as remains accessible.

6 Connect the ring terminals to the battery posts – red to positive and black to negative.

7 Insert the master fuse – your power panel is now live and ready to use.

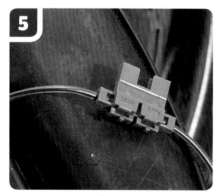

Having an auxiliary power source that is only 'live' with the ignition on is advantageous as it avoids the possibility of flattening the battery by inadvertently leaving an accessory powered up. The 'Fuzeblock' is an easily installed solution to this problem and gives the flexibility of delivering power of a higher current than would normally be available via the bike's CAN-bus system; it is very useful for accessories such as compressors or heated clothing. The power provided by the Fuzeblock can be toggled to either permanently live or ignition-switched simply by the placement of the fuse protecting that outlet.

1 Install the appropriate crimp terminals to the accessory socket or the CAN-bus splitter cable, or tap into the accessory socket power lead.
2 Cut a length of twin-core red/black 2mm² cable sufficient to reach the battery from the Fuzeblock's mounting point. Install an in-line fuse holder (minus the fuse for the moment) in the red 2mm² cable, in an accessible position close to the battery.
3 Install 6mm ring terminals at each end to connect to the fuse panel and the battery posts, red to the positive (+ve) and black to the negative (−ve) terminals of the battery.
4 Mount the Fuzeblock in its chosen location.
5 Connect the main power cables from the battery to the Fuzeblock.
6 Connect the trigger supply from the CAN-bus cable or accessory socket power supply to the Fuzeblock.
7 Install the fuse into the main fuse holder – the Fuzeblock is now live and switched by the CAN-bus.
8 Refit the Fuzeblock's cover and fix the unit in place.

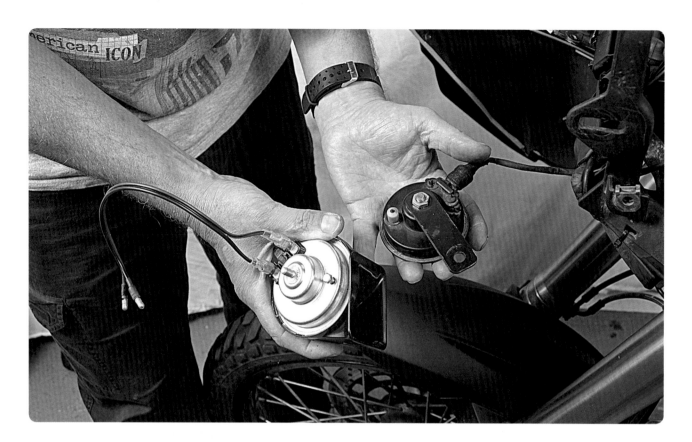

The horn fitted to most motorcycles is generally quite feeble compared with those of most cars. This is very obvious in urban third world traffic, where the sound you will hear most frequently is the frantic blaring of horns! In these situations, there will be occasions when you need to announce your presence with a quick toot of the horn, but it has to be heard above the general cacophany. Thankfully, fitment of a louder horn is a quick and easy modification, requiring little time.

1 Remove the original horn unit and disconnect the wiring that connects it to the main loom.
2 Replace the connectors as required, adding extra cable if necessary.
3 Install the new horn unit, making sure it fits in the available space and does not foul any other body panels.
4 Reconnect the wiring harness and have a toot!

Without doubt one of the accessories that has grown significantly in popularity in recen years is on-board navigation using GPS (global positioning system) technology. There are many different types of GPS receiver units available, but clearly using one designed for a motorcycle will best serve your purpose.

A GPS unit will usually be shipped with its own cradle and a universal mounting kit, but by their nature these can sometimes limit the opportunities for positioning the receiver in the best position to suit you. High-end mounting systems such as the Z-Technik unit give three-dimensional flexibility and can allow the receiver to be placed in virtually any position. This is especially useful if you have a tank bag or bar bag that might compromise access to, or visibility of, the area around the handlebar clamps.

Selecting the right GPS receiver is therefore important. High-end models will have Bluetooth functionality, allowing wireless communication with your intercom, your mobile phone and even your helmet, if that has Bluetooth capability.

If you are fitting a full system you will need to access power somewhere (see the section on fitting an auxiliary fuse panel, pages 139–140) so have your electrical tools – wire strippers, crimping pliers, etc, to hand, and be sure to read the manufacturer's installation suggestions.

1   Loosely fit the mount clamp on the handlebars so that the mounting arm and cradle do not foul the screen or block your view of the instrument panel.
2   Remove any bodywork or panels required to access the power source and make the necessary connections. If you are not using an auxiliary power panel, remember to use a fuse to protect your wiring.
3   Secure the power cable to the existing harness with cable ties, ensuring it is not chafing or rubbing, and that there are no tight spots when you turn the handlebars.
4   Plug the power supply into the mount, install the GPS unit into its cradle and turn on.

This project can be extremely rewarding as long as there is a convenient location to mount the control unit. The KTM 990 has a very useful cubbyhole located between the filler caps which is large enough for most intercom units, and it is very conveniently placed next to the fuse panel too. The BMW R1200GS has a small space in the tool tray under the seat that is often used, and the F800GS has a space under the tailpiece, or if that is occupied by an alarm unit there is a small space underneath the dummy tank cover.

When choosing where to mount the unit remember that you will need access to it to be able to make adjustments to volume, voice level, etc, as well as routing the rider and pillion output cables to convenient positions on the bike. The ideal connection to the bike's power supply will be via an auxiliary fuse panel, but equally you can power it from a bespoke connector in the spare accessory socket, or tap into either a switched live feed or an auxiliary power socket as described on the facing page. Whatever supply you elect to use, it must be protected by an appropriately rated fuse.

1 Locate the mounting point, and place the control unit in position.
2 Remove any bodywork required, and run the power cable to your selected outlet and make it secure with cable ties.
3 Examine where the output cables will be best placed and run them alongside any existing cabling, securing them with cable ties where necessary.
4 Visually check the final placement for potential chafing or tightness in the cables.
5 If you are installing auxiliary components such as an MP3 player or a Bluetooth module, take this opportunity to run any cables to the accessory's mounting point.
6 Connect the power cables to the fused supply or an appropriate alternative power supply.
7 Make a final test for functionality before refitting bodywork.

An auxiliary power outlet is one of the most useful modifications you can make to an ADV bike, allowing you to power accessories and in some cases even use a charging system without having direct access to the battery. If you have room, installing both types (lighter socket and DIN/Hella) gives even more flexibility.

Decide if you need to have the socket live all the time or if a switched feed best suits your needs. Leaving an accessory charger running overnight, or when the bike is unattended, might sound useful but will be highly inconvenient if you return to a flat battery. Marine sockets are great for external use as they are designed to be waterproof.

1 Identify a suitable location for the outlet – ideally in the instrument binnacle, on a side panel by the seat or even under the seat if there is space. On the bike shown, the relocation of the tool kit provided an ideal location for an under-seat socket.

2 Once you have decided on a suitable location, check there will be sufficient clearance to plug in any adapters you may wish to use. This is especially important with instrument-mounted sockets where the handlebars or hand guards can get close to the instruments on full lock. If required, make a suitably sized hole in the panel where the socket will be installed using a hole saw or a cone-cutter.

3 Locate a suitable power source – the battery's positive terminal or the live terminal of the starter motor relay. Measure and cut a generous length of correctly rated cable – try to route the cable alongside the existing loom.

4 Install an in-line fuse holder as close to the power supply as is practical. Do not insert the fuse at this time. Ensure any soldered joints are correctly insulated.

5 Install the power outlet and connect using the appropriate crimped connectors.

6 Crimp correctly sized ring terminal connectors on to the cable and connect to the power supply. The ground or earth cable can be connected to the negative terminal of the battery or to a suitable part of the chassis.

7 Install the fuse to complete the circuit. Be sure to use a sufficiently rated fuse – 15A should be sufficient for most accessories.

Auxiliary lights are often the first accessory fitted to the majority of ADV bikes. Sometimes they are needed because the original lighting system leaves something to be desired, while at other times additional lighting will give the confidence of greater conspicuousness or 'presence', allowing the rider to be much more visible to other road users.

Various accessories are available in the marketplace, but without doubt the best results will be achieved by using kits that have been designed for your particular motorcycle. Using such a kit assures you that everything will fit, and generally the end result will be aesthetically pleasing as well as being reliable and functional.

The first decision to be made will be how to provide power for the lights. If you have a CAN-bus system then your options are somewhat limited by the capacity of the system, and whether your bike has an available access point in the wiring loom. In this instance the simplest solution is to use a switching relay, triggered by the dipped-beam circuit, which will ensure that the auxiliary lights turn off with

the principal light. Auxiliary lighting consumes a lot of power, and may need more power than the alternator on some motorcycles can actually supply. Taking too much power from the bike will very quickly flatten the battery and may also overheat cabling that is not designed to carry high current loads, so fitting a switch to the trigger circuit is advisable to allow the extra lights to be turned off when not required, or if you need to give maximum charging current to the battery. If you are in danger of using too much power, consider using an alternative lighting system such as high-intensity discharge (HID) lights, which give greater light output but use less power.

Using a custom-designed mounting bar saves you the headache of trying to work out how to mount the lights, and gives you the confidence that you will not need to start fabricating other items to make it all work. As with all kits, take the time to read the instructions, and familiarise yourself with the contents, identifying the different parts and components, and where they will go on the bike. If you need to create a power source, then locate suitable points for routing the

supply cable and mounting the switching relay. If you have already installed an auxiliary fused power panel (see pages 139–140) then this can be the power source rather than a direct connection to the battery. You may need to remove parts of your bike's bodywork, so be sure to tackle this task in a good working space, with plenty of room to move around the bike.

All electrical accessories must be grounded or earthed to complete the circuit back to the battery. Check your lights to determine what system they use for grounding – some light units rely upon their mounting point to the chassis, while others will have a separate cable to ground. The type with a separate ground wire is particularly suitable as it allows the fitment of lights to plastic or composite body panels which do not earth back to the chassis. The power needed to trigger the relay will be coming from 'tapped' points in the headlight dipped-beam circuit, which will require the use of a soldering iron, as will the feed from the relay to the lights which divides into two to provide individual power supplies for each light unit.

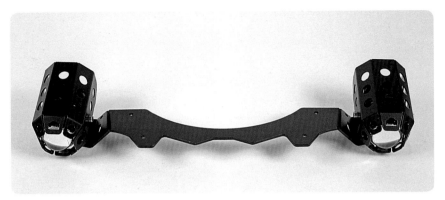

Materials

- ■ Light mounting bar and fixings
- ■ Auxiliary lights
- ■ Cable – twin-core 10 amp (red and black)
- ■ Cable – single-core 3 amp
- ■ 12v switching relay
- ■ Cable ties
- ■ In-line fuse holder
- ■ Insulating tape

Tools

- ■ Wire clippers
- ■ Crimp terminals – 6mm ring
- ■ Crimp terminals – female spade
- ■ Crimp terminals – 6.3mm piggyback
- ■ Crimping pliers
- ■ Soldering iron and solder

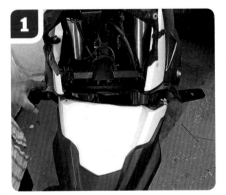

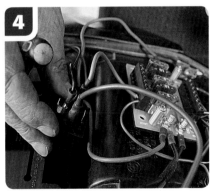

1 Offer up the mounting bar to visualise how it will be fitted on the bike.

2 Remove any bodywork necessary to access the power points and route the supply cables.

3 Select the point in the wiring loom to 'tap' the supply for the switching relay and identify routes for the power supply cable and relay trigger cables, and the location for the relay.

4 Identify the terminals on the relay. If they are ISO standard, each terminal will be numbered: 85 and 86 are the trigger terminals, and 30 and 87 are the power terminals.

5 Estimate the cable length (twin-core, red, $2mm^2$ – 10A) from the battery to the relay, then on to auxiliary light no. 1, add another 20cm and cut to length.

6 Estimate the cable length (red/black twin-core, $2mm^2$ – 10A) between light no. 1 and light no. 2, add another 30–40cm and cut to length. Estimate the cable length (single-core $1mm^2$ – 3A) between the dipped-beam wiring tap point and the relay, add another 20–30cm and cut to length.

7 Check the bike's wiring diagram to identify a suitable current source to trigger the relay. If you need your auxiliary lights to come on with the headlamp, then you can tap into the dipped-beam power feed. Having identified the wire that will supply the trigger for the relay, it is necessary to create the wire taps. Where possible it is simplest to use a 'piggyback' crimped connector to take a feed, otherwise you will need to make a soldered connection. Separate the appropriate wire from the loom bundle and gently score around it with a sharp knife, taking care not to cut the core of the cable. Pull back the insulating sheath to reveal about 5mm of the wire core. Strip about 1cm of insulation from the tap wire and wrap the core of the tap wire around the core of the headlamp's power wire. Join the two cables using the soldering iron and solder, making sure that the solder flows well into the wire.

8 Insulate the join with heat-shrink tubing or electrical insulation tape, then re-wrap the cables back into the loom.

9 Adhesive linen tape is ideal as its glue does not degrade over time, as some PVC tapes do. Run it back to the relay, using zip ties to secure it to the main loom bundle.

10 Run the length of red/black twin-core 2mm^2 (10A) wire (prepared in step 5) from the battery via the relay to light no. 1 and zip-tie loosely into place, leaving sufficient cable to trim to the correct length when making the final fitment of the lights. At the relay, separate the two cores and cut the red cable ready to accept the crimp connectors for the relay.

11 At a convenient and accessible point close to the battery, separate the red and black cable cores and install an in-line fuse holder into the red cable, making sure there is enough cable left to reach the battery posts before crimping ring terminals ready to connect to the battery terminals. Do not insert a fuse at this stage.

12 Apply crimp terminals to each cut end of the red cable at the relay and connect to terminals 30 and 87. Apply a crimp connector to the end of the tap wire

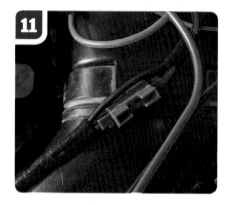

and connect to terminal 85, and use an appropriate length of black 3A wire with crimped connectors to connect terminal 86 to the negative terminal of the battery, or to a ground point on the chassis if more convenient.

13 Using the same soldering technique as described in step 7, 'tee' the second piece of red/black twin-core 2mm² (10A) cable into the first at a convenient place, so that it can follow the line of the mounting bar or sub-frame to deliver power to light no. 2. Again, insulate the join with linen tape, and secure the wire with zip ties.

14 Crimp on the appropriate terminals to connect to the second auxiliary light.

15 Re-install any bodywork required but leave the relay accessible, ready for connection of the trigger and power wires and final insertion of the fuse.

16 Install the auxiliary light units on to the light bar, including any protective shrouds. Do not overtighten at this stage.

17 Route the cables through the bodywork and the light mounting bar, to terminate close to each light unit. Crimp the appropriate connector to the end of each cable.

18 Connect the appropriate cables to the bulb and install into the light housing.

19 Fit the rubber sealing boot to the back of the light housing to protect the bulb and connections, and protect the exposed cables with sheathing or corrugated trunking.

20 Tighten the mounting screws of the light units sufficiently to allow adjustment.

21 Complete the circuit by inserting the fuse into its holder. With the bike switched on and running, the auxiliary lights will come on with the dipped beam.

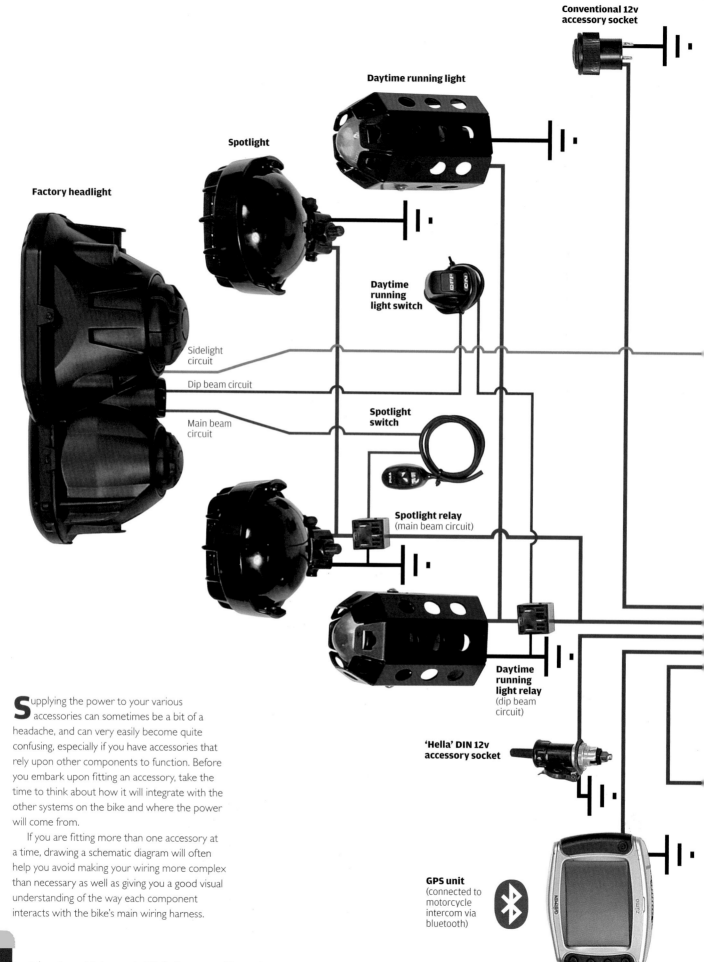

Conventional 12v accessory socket

Daytime running light

Spotlight

Factory headlight

Daytime running light switch

Sidelight circuit

Dip beam circuit

Main beam circuit

Spotlight switch

Spotlight relay
(main beam circuit)

Daytime running light relay
(dip beam circuit)

'Hella' DIN 12v accessory socket

GPS unit
(connected to motorcycle intercom via bluetooth)

Supplying the power to your various accessories can sometimes be a bit of a headache, and can very easily become quite confusing, especially if you have accessories that rely upon other components to function. Before you embark upon fitting an accessory, take the time to think about how it will integrate with the other systems on the bike and where the power will come from.

If you are fitting more than one accessory at a time, drawing a schematic diagram will often help you avoid making your wiring more complex than necessary as well as giving you a good visual understanding of the way each component interacts with the bike's main wiring harness.

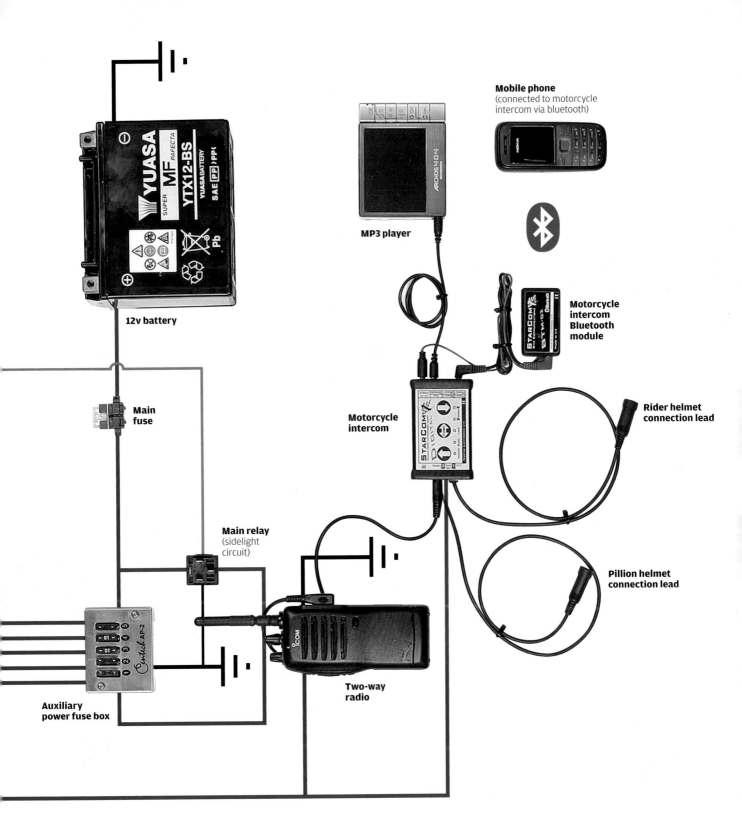

12v battery

Main fuse

Main relay
(sidelight circuit)

Auxiliary power fuse box

MP3 player

Mobile phone
(connected to motorcycle intercom via bluetooth)

Motorcycle intercom Bluetooth module

Motorcycle intercom

Rider helmet connection lead

Pillion helmet connection lead

Two-way radio

Repairs

■ Author

ne of the main fears for newcomers to ADV riding is the prospect of being stranded at the roadside. Facing this will be more daunting in a foreign or hostile environment where no obvious help is within reach, and in these circumstances the harsh reality is that you will have to rely upon your own resourcefulness to extricate yourself from whatever situation you find yourself in. the actions you will need to take will depend on the extent of the problem, but being able to make a temporary fix will allow you to limp to the nearest populated area to get a proper repair done.

Having a skill as simple as being able to fix a puncture can literally be a lifesaver but, more importantly, having the confidence in your own ability to be able to deal with problems will make your tour experience so much better. One of the hardest things to master is the ability to keep a cool head. No problem has ever been eased or solved by flapping around – indeed worrying about something consumes a huge amount of emotional energy and saps your confidence – so making a calm assessment of your situation will be the first step of the repair.

TOP 10 ROADSIDE PROBLEMS

1 Crash damage

2 Electrical pitfalls

3 Starting problems

4 Supporting the bike

5   Removing wheels

6   Punctures

7   Wheel bearing failure

8   Brake pad failure

9   Chain damage

10   Overheating

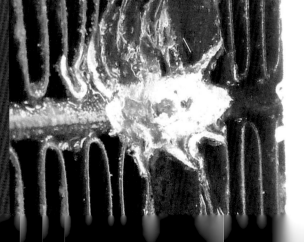

↑ **Thankfully the only thing injured here was pride!**
📷 Author

If you are riding off-road, it is almost inevitable that at some time or other you will fall off or drop the bike. Hopefully you will have prepared for this eventuality by fitting some sort of crash protection, but the risk of damage to the bike will always be there.

Steering system

One of the most common falls comes from the front end 'tucking in' on a loose surface or getting crossed up in a slippery rut with the steering at full lock. If the front end then hits something solid or jams in the rut, the momentum of the bike will try to force the wheel beyond the limit of the steering lock. There can be a terrific amount of force behind this and in extreme circumstances the frame or fork legs could be distorted. Happily this kind of damage is a rare occurrence and the more usual result is the fork stanchions twisting in the yoke or 'triple-tree'. Thankfully this always looks worse than it is and, unless the wheel itself is damaged, can be quite easily resolved.

Once you have picked up the bike and got back to level ground, you will probably see quite a dramatic deflection. If you are lucky you might just be able to hold the wheel between your knees and jerk it back into alignment with the handlebars, but if you can do that the yoke pinch bolts

are probably too loose – which may have contributed to the original problem. With the bike on either the side stand or the main stand, slightly loosen off the handlebar clamp bolts, the main axle and clamp nuts, and the yoke pinch bolts – but not so much that the forks slip through the yokes – and apply full lock opposite to the twist. Then take the front wheel in both hands and try to turn it against the lock-stop until the twist is corrected. You can apply a surprising amount of force in this way so it should not be too difficult to get it all to align.

When you have corrected the deflection, nip up the lower yoke pinch bolts and take a look at the steering again, repeating the operation until the steering is straight. Nip up the remaining bolts on the top yoke and the handlebar clamp and then bounce the forks up and down vigorously while holding the front brake. This relieves any tension between the axle clamps and allows everything to settle back into its natural position.

The final stage is to retighten all the fasteners, starting with the axle pinch bolts followed by the axle nut, the lower yoke pinch bolts followed by the top yoke pinch bolts, and finally the handlebar clamps. Give the front wheel a quick spin to ensure that it turns freely and continue your journey.

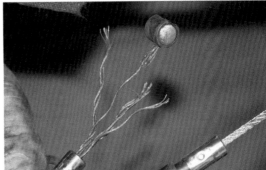

← ← **This simple device could save a broken foot lever.**
📷 Touratech

← **This cable really is hanging on by a thread!**
📷 Author

Steel and aluminium levers

The *lowside* is another common fall, either from the rear wheel stepping out under power or the front wheel 'washing out' in a turn. Here the bike generally falls with the forks on opposite lock, which can damage gearchange and footbrake levers as well as handlebars. These items can be made of either steel or alloy and both types can be bent or distorted, but the different materials need different approaches to straighten them.

A steel lever is generally quite easy to straighten as long as the metal has not cracked or been fatigued from a previous bend. It can normally be 'persuaded' back into shape either with a lever or by tapping it gently with a hammer, but care must be taken to support it and not apply excess stresses to the splined shaft it is attached to. If the steel cannot be straightened cold, then a campfire will usually provide sufficient heat to make it malleable enough to be straightened.

Straightening a forged aluminium lever needs a somewhat different approach. Aluminium has a different metallic structure from steel, and behaves very differently under the stress of being bent. Raw or natural aluminium is quite soft and ductile, but the heat of the forging process changes its metallic crystalline structure, making it much more rigid and harder to bend. When it is bent, however, micro-cracks are formed in the crystalline structure of the metal, making it significantly weaker, and far less flexible. The reality of this is that the lever will bend relatively easily on the first occasion, but it is very likely to break if you try to bend it back to its original shape.

Heat-treating or annealing the aluminium will restore much of its softness and ductility and will give you a good chance of straightening the bend. Again this can be achieved over a campfire, but at 600°C aluminium has a much lower melting point than steel, and it will transform from solid to liquid without glowing like steel, so great care must be taken to prevent this happening. Aluminium will anneal at 400°C, which happens to be the temperature at which hand soap burns, so smearing soap on the lever and heating it until it burns off will give a perfectly annealed lever that can be gently reshaped once it has cooled down.

Control cables

A broken control cable need not be the disaster it might seem at first. Bowden cable, as it is properly known, is pretty much universal and the various components should be readily available just about anywhere. If you simply lose a nipple, then use a solderless screw-fit replacement. Various sizes and configurations are available and if they are properly fitted they are just as strong as an original cable, and it is certainly worth keeping a couple in your tool kit as a 'get-you-home' measure. If you are stuck without a screw-nipple, then a small pair of vice grips can be used on the end of a clutch cable threaded through the lever. Universal cable, usually used for a pedal cycle's derailleur gear, is long and thin, can be cut with a pair of pliers and in an emergency can generally be persuaded to do most things a thicker cable should do.

⬇ **An easily achieved roadside repair – if you have grips!**
📷 Rob Herrera

➜ In an emergency, any repair is a good repair...
📷 Tami Rowell

Fuel tank

Cracking or holing a fuel tank is never a good thing, especially if you have a full fuel load. If you are overlanding, the priority here must be to save as much fuel as possible. If possible, drain the tank via the fuel tap, or catch the leak with a jug and save it in a jerry can or another bike's fuel tank, or rest the bike on its side so that the hole is uppermost. Once you have emptied the tank the repair can start.

A small hole in either a metal tank or a plastic tank can be sealed using a self-tapping screw and a sealing washer of some sort, ideally a small 'O' ring, but even a puncture repair patch will do the same job. Larger holes or cracks in a plastic tank can be repaired using a soldering iron or a heat gun and a supply of 'filler' – a plastic bottle top is ideal for this task. A metal tank with a crack can be effectively sealed using a

fast-setting epoxy adhesive, but the surface of the repair must be scrupulously clean and well-keyed to ensure adequate adhesion. In an absolute emergency, and if you do not have any suitable tools, rub some hand soap into the crack or hole. The petrol will react with the soap to produce a hard gum-like material that will seal up the leak. Use a strip of duct tape to reinforce the soap plug and make a more permanent repair as soon as is practical.

Frame

An ADV bike will take a tremendous pounding on the trail, and a crack or break in the frame might be a result of a heavy spill or from simply overloading the bike. Thankfully the structurally important parts of the chassis are generally engineered with a significant margin of safety. However, this usually means that any fracture you find will probably be on a secondary part of the chassis such as a rear sub-frame or a luggage rack.

Taking a look at the sub-frame assembly of the bike reveals how it gains its strength, and also where the weak points are, although it might not be immediately obvious. Any part of the frame can quickly become fatigued, especially when the structure is subjected to the stress of vibration and repeated micro-bending caused by severe road undulation. If the loads are above a certain threshold, microscopic cracks can begin to form on the tubular framework and will eventually reach a critical size, growing quickly to become a complete fracture. The shape of the framework significantly determines fatigue potential, and any drillings or holes will lead to increased local stresses where fatigue cracks can begin to show. Square holes

➜ Overloading probably caused this failure.
📷 Andreas Hülsmann

or sharp corners concentrate and focus stresses, leading to increased fatigue potential, so round holes and smooth weld transitions or fillets will increase the fatigue strength of the structure and ultimately reduce the risk of failure. First and foremost, though, is the need to avoid overloading the weakest part of the structure – it is strongest at its point of triangulation.

If you do find a crack, it is imperative to assess the damage and determine whether it will continue to be a risk to the integrity of the motorcycle. The first step is to limit any further damage that the fracture area might sustain. For example, if the fracture is in a member that is under compressive strain, it can be secured with duct tape to stop the fractured ends clashing against each other any more than necessary. If the fracture is in tensile strain, then it can be 'splinted' with a section of angle steel and clamped with steel hose clips. Obviously this type of temporary repair will be very weak and cannot be subjected to high levels of stress, so ride gently and take the earliest opportunity to have it properly repaired.

If the fracture is more significant, for example a cracked steering head or swing-arm pivot, then great care must be taken not to make the damage worse. In certain circumstances a ratchet strap can be used to pull the fracture back together, and if it can be held tight enough this might be all you need to get back to civilisation for a properly welded repair.

Once you get back to the welding shop, be sure to disconnect your alternator before letting anyone get close to it with a welding machine – the current produced in welding, and which also flows through the bike's chassis, is very high and can easily disrupt or damage the components in the rectifier/regulator unit. Modern fuel-injected bikes will have an ECU, the central 'brain' that controls the electronic workings of the bike's engine and ancillaries, and this can also be fragile when exposed to high currents, so, for peace of mind, take five minutes to disconnect the ECU as well.

↑ **A crude but effective repair.**
📷 Luke Deikis

← **Health and safety rules are different the world over!**
📷 Author

Some of the most difficult problems to diagnose occur in electrical systems. Some problems, such as an intermittent fault caused by a poor contact, can be very hard to track down.

Fuses

If a component or an accessory suddenly stops working, the first thing to check is the fuse protecting its supply circuit. If the fuse has blown then something is wrong with that circuit; as fuses will not generally blow without good reason, you must find the cause of the failure before simply replacing it, otherwise the new fuse will just blow immediately too.

Look for the obvious: a chafe in the loom can expose individual cables and allow current to short-circuit to the chassis. One classic point for this to happen is at the steering head, where the constant movement of the handlebars can allow a badly placed or insecure wiring harness to rub against the chassis. Other bulky parts of the loom sometimes have to pass over chassis rails and under the seat, so it is all too easy for a wire to become trapped and crushed under the seat mounting. If the fuse is intact, check that you have power at the accessory. If you have voltage at its terminals, then the accessory or component has probably failed. No voltage at the terminals indicates a break in the power supply somewhere, but one without a current leakage to ground. Check for loose or disconnected connectors, or a cable chafed against a plastic (non-conducting) body part.

Connectors

Less obvious failure can be caused by almost any electrical connection on the bike, especially if it is used in arduous conditions. The combination of moisture and electricity creates the perfect environment for galvanic corrosion, which is responsible for the nasty green deposits that can sometimes be found in the wiring loom's connector blocks. Once established, this corrosion can cause a variety of issues, some of which can be difficult to identify, especially as the symptoms can be intermittent. In some cases, the corrosion of the brass connectors can be so great that the 'verdigris' – a by-product of the corrosion process – can build up sufficiently to break electrical contact. A more insidious manifestation is the presence of just enough corrosion to create a point of electrical resistance within the connector block itself.

Electrical resistance in any circuit will generate heat, and the higher the resistance the more heat will be produced. In the worst case, there can be sufficient heat to completely melt the connector block and cable insulation, allowing a direct short and creating a very real risk of fire. On the other hand, low resistance and a small amount of heat might distort the connector just enough to break the circuit temporarily and cause an intermittent problem. Corroded connectors can be cleaned up with a little emery paper or a small file, while citric acid or lemon juice will do a good job of removing corrosion in less accessible connectors. Rinse well with water, then apply copious quantities of WD40 or similar on reassembly to hold further corrosion at bay.

→ **Be aware of any sharp edges close to a cable.**
📷 Author

→→ **Corrosion and fatigue caused this soldered joint to fail.**
📷 Author

→→ **This connector overheated to a critical level owing to corrosion.**
📷 Author

Resolving electrical problems can be tricky, especially if the fault is intermittent, but look for the obvious causes first. If an accessory stops working, have a look at the closest part of the wiring harness; it could have been trapped somewhere or a connector might simply have popped apart. Water getting into the electrics is also a common problem, especially in the ignition circuit where the high-voltage supply to the spark plugs needs very little excuse to find an easier way to earth!

Handlebar switches

Handlebar switches are exposed to virtually every adverse condition a motorcycle will encounter, yet they are still expected to function properly each time they are used. The switchgear used on older bikes does not have as much internal protection as more modern models, but both types will benefit from lubrication to keep them moving smoothly. On older bikes switchgear can be opened up to reveal the various sliding connectors inside. Take care not to displace any of the small springs or levers and use WD40 or a similar dry-film aerosol lubricant to flood the switch mechanism. This will displace any accumulated debris and also lubricate the pivots and sliders while providing a degree of waterproofing. On more modern bikes, the low current demand of CAN-bus-controlled systems means that smaller sealed micro-switch modules can be used inside the main switch body. Periodic application of WD40 will help keep the switch actuator rockers operating smoothly and efficiently.

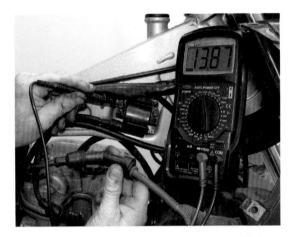
← **Using a test meter can highlight potential problems.**
📷 Haynes

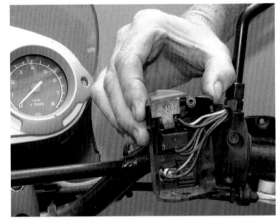
← **Semi-sealed switchgear is less likely to fail.**
📷 Haynes

← **Fine dust can penetrate anywhere.**
📷 Robert Wicks

→ The side-stand cut-out switch is particularly exposed to damage.
📷 Haynes

Battery depletion

A common problem is battery failure or depletion, and identifying the cause of the failure is the first step in resolving the issue. If you ride with a lot of accessories – such as heated grips, clothing and auxiliary lighting – in operation, you might use more electrical power than the alternator can supply.

Under normal running, the bike's alternator will supply sufficient current to power basic systems such as the ignition, ECU (engine control unit) and daylight running lights, and to keep the battery fully charged. There will also be a limited amount of 'spare' power for accessories such as GPS or heated grips, but if you take more than the alternator can supply the battery will have to provide the shortfall. This is acceptable for short periods of time, as the alternator will restore charge level once the accessories are switched off, but running for too long from your battery's reserve can soon leave you with insufficient power and a flat battery.

Side-stand switch

On any motorcycle, the side-stand cut-out switch is very vulnerable to damage or malfunction, and it can be the cause of some peculiar and intermittent faults that may not always be obviously attributable to it. As an example, if the switch gets wet during a water crossing, it may give continuity problems. However, when the switch dries, electrical continuity is restored and the problem disappears. The switch can also cause a misfire if the retracting spring does not hold the stand fully closed when the bike is moving. Bumpy terrain might allow it to move enough to actuate the switch momentarily and cut ignition, giving the impression of a misfire, which will obviously be very difficult to track down when the bike is at a standstill.

The switch can either be service maintained and disassembled to seal it from external elements, or it can be removed altogether, thus completely eliminating the possibility of it causing a fault. If removing the switch, you will need to check its functionality – whether it is open or closed to enable the ignition – and then either isolate or connect the terminals accordingly. Disabling the side-stand switch like this allows the motorcycle to run with the stand deployed, so ultimate diligence will be required to ensure that the stand is properly retracted before riding away. Remember that this is an emergency solution, and that for safety's sake the functionality of the switch must be restored as soon as practicable.

Starting any bike with a flat battery can be a challenge. Some electronic ignition and fuel injection circuits require a minimum voltage before they can work, and many modern bikes are not equipped with a kick-start lever, relying solely upon the electric starter motor to get the engine running.

A bump start is perhaps the easiest to try first, especially if you have a downhill gradient to help! If the bike is well loaded, then it is probably best to take the luggage off, as you will need the bike to be as light as possible for the next stage. Turn off all accessories, and if you have daylight running lights disconnect the bulb connector if you can reach it. Select second or third gear and make sure the kill switch is set to ON. Pull in the clutch lever and get a willing helper to push you, or roll down the hill to a reasonable speed. Once you have built up a little momentum, let out the clutch sharply to get the engine turning and hopefully started. If you are on a loose surface use a higher gear and 'bump' your bodyweight on to the saddle as you declutch, maximising road contact and rear-wheel grip. Be ready to pull the clutch in again to prevent the bike running away with you when it does start.

This manoeuvre is physically very demanding, especially if you do not have anyone to help you push, so try to make the most of your effort. If the back wheel just locks up, then select a higher gear and try again. Once the engine is running *do not turn it off!* Leaving the bike to idle while you reload your luggage will help restore the battery's charge, and when you eventually get back on the road keep as many accessories as possible disconnected for as long as possible to allow the battery to recharge fully.

If bump-starting fails, then starting the bike with jump leads or booster cables might be the only remaining option. This emergency starting method involves connecting a second vehicle's battery directly to your motorcycle's flat battery by means of a set of heavy-duty cables. This can be problematic if the battery is stowed in an awkward location that requires the removal of some body panels to gain access.

Make sure the ignition is switched off on both vehicles. Then, once you have access to the battery's terminals, attach the red booster lead first to the positive terminal of the flat battery. Taking care not to let the other end of the cable touch any part of the bodywork or chassis, connect it to the positive terminal of the donor battery. The negative or black leads can now be attached. Again, starting with the bike with the flat battery, first connect the lead to the negative terminal of the battery, and then to the negative terminal of the second vehicle. Start the second vehicle's engine and let it run at a fast idle to build up a good initial charge in both batteries. After a couple of minutes try to start your bike as normal. If the bike starts, then letting it run for a few more minutes will help equalise the charge between batteries and minimise sparking or voltage surges as the cables are disconnected. If the bike does not start first time, then leave both batteries connected to allow as much charge as possible to get to the flat battery. Be aware that repeated attempts to start the bike will make the booster cables and clamps quite hot, so be careful when disconnecting them.

← **In the event that you are unable to jump-start your bike from another vehicle, and attempts to bump-start fail, you may be forced to resort to more basic methods of reaching your destination. This approach might raise an eyebrow with the police in some countries...**
📷 Thorvaldur Orn Kristmundsson

Battery failure

Riding in very hot weather can seriously affect conventional lead/acid batteries, as high temperatures can accelerate electrolyte loss through evaporation. If discovered early enough this situation can be recovered by refilling the battery with distilled water, but in all circumstances the life of any battery is seriously compromised by running it dry. In an emergency tap water can be used to top up the battery, but its mineral and salt content will significantly alter the chemical balance of the electrolyte and can seriously reduce the battery's capacity, as well as its life.

The worst fate a battery can endure is continual overcharging. This will invariably be as a result of the failure of the voltage rectifier/regulator (VRR) unit, leading to uncontrolled voltage and current being directed into the battery. This level of voltage can heat up a battery very quickly, and can quite easily boil it dry, destroying it in the process. The VRR can fail unpredictably, and this will generally be because of overheating resulting from the high resistances caused by poor or corroded connections from the alternator, or simply due to a component failure within the VRR itself.

If this happens, the only practical solution would be to source a fully charged 12v battery and temporarily disconnect the alternator to prevent it being overcharged as well. With every unnecessary ancillary item disconnected, the bike will run for as long as the battery can power the ignition. Hopefully this will be far enough to get you somewhere to make a repair, or use a phone.

Fuel flooding

If you have trouble starting the bike, and it does not respond to cranking or turning on the starter motor, it is possible that the spark plugs may have been wetted by excess fuel pumped into the cylinder by the carburettor or fuel injection system – a problem more commonly known as 'flooding'. This will be very evident from the strong smell of fuel from the exhaust, so no smoking while doing this job! Thankfully, fuel injection systems are much less prone to this problem than carburettor engines, but in either event the recovery is relatively simple.

Conventionally, cranking a carburettor engine with the throttle held wide open will allow maximum airflow through the engine, flushing out the excess fuel via the exhaust port. For an injected engine, it is imperative to crank the engine, but with the throttle closed, letting the engine's electronics sort out the fuelling. In either case, however, pumping or twisting the throttle during this process will only pour more fuel into the cylinders, making the problem worse. If the injected engine is still not responding, then some ECUs have a 'clear cylinder' mode engaged if 'wide-open throttle' is applied during start-up. This setting defeats the injection system and allows the engine to be cranked with no fuel flow, effectively venting the cylinders of the excess fuel.

↑ An 'intelligent' charger can indicate a failing battery.
📷 Author

➡ A spark plug this dark is never a good sign.
📷 Author

In extreme circumstances, you may not be able to crank the engine over enough to clear the liquid fuel from the cylinder. The only way to resolve this situation is by removing the spark plug from the cylinder and cranking the engine sufficiently to blow the liquid fuel out of the spark-plug hole. With zero compression, the engine will turn over very quickly and easily, and thankfully with little strain on the battery. Once the fuel has been ejected, let the cylinder 'breathe' for a few minutes, to help evaporate the last of the excess fuel. Use this time to dry and clean the spark plug/s to be sure of a healthy spark when refitted. Do the same to the plug lead and plug cap, and if you have a can of water dispersant spray use some inside the cap and on the leads. Be sure not to let any debris fall into the cylinder while the plug is removed. Once the plug is refitted (remember, hand-tight plus another quarter turn!), the engine should start as normal.

↑ **This drowned Honda did restart – eventually.**
📷 Author

Water flooding

If you are planning any river or long water crossings, there is a possibility that at some stage you will get water in your engine, or even be unfortunate enough to submerge the bike completely. This might seem like an utter disaster, but it is not the end of the world...

Once the bike is back on dry land, remove any luggage to make it easier to move the bike, and the restarting process can begin. Water can – and will – get everywhere, so you will be doing a fair amount of mopping and drying before anything else. The techniques involved are pretty much the same whatever bike you ride, although air intakes and filters may be in different locations and may require a slightly different approach.

Thankfully, very little water is likely to have got past the air filter and into the combustion chamber but, even so, never try to clear the bike straight away. If you have more than a few cubic centimetres of water in the engine and try to crank it over with the starter, there is a real danger of creating a hydraulic lock within the cylinder that is capable of bending a con rod – that will mean an expensive repair bill and possibly even the end of your tour.

← **Always know how high your air intake is before attempting a deep-water crossing.**
📷 Touratech

If your bike has been completely submerged, then *all* possibilities for water intrusion must be investigated, which means gaining access to most of the top half of the bike. Getting it running again will take a couple of hours, depending on how easy access is, so consider the impact that this delay will have on the remainder of your day's journey.

With the bike upright and on firm ground, locate and remove the spark plug/s, removing the fuel tank if necessary. If the plugs are wet, blow as much water out of them as possible, then put them to one side to dry. Locate and remove the air filter, shake out any excess water and put it to dry with the spark plugs, mopping out the air box if necessary. Any water in the carburettor can be drained by removing the drain screw or cap on the bottom of the float-bowl – if you have not removed the tank at this point, be sure that the fuel tap is closed first!

Using the starter motor, crank the engine for a good 10–15 seconds to clear any water from the cylinder bores. If you only have a kick-starter, then 15 or 20 vigorous kicks should be enough to do the same.

If you have any water-dispersant spray then now would be a good time to spray it liberally over any exposed or wet electrics, concentrating especially on the spark-plug caps and lead. Put the plug back into the plug cap and turn the engine over again, with the plug earthed to the engine casing to check for a spark – this also helps expel any remaining water from the bore. Refit the spark plug to the cylinder head and attach the plug cap. Replace the dried air filter and refit the tank. The fuel in your tank *should* be OK, but any water that has managed to get inside will settle at the lowest part of the tank, as it is heavier than the fuel. Water can be purged via the fuel tap by disconnecting the fuel line and draining a little fuel – any water present will be seen as globules in the bottom of the fuel. Reconnect the fuel line and allow the carburettor to fill with clean fuel. With fingers crossed, take a deep breath and hit the starter button – the engine should start!

Once you have started the engine, leave it running for a good 15–20 minutes to warm through, then check the engine oil for any signs of water contamination. When the motor is hot, any water that has managed to get into the engine casings will combine with oil in a thick creamy-coloured emulsion which will be seen underneath the oil filler cap and around the filler neck. If you see any sign of contamination then you must change the oil as soon as possible, because the emulsified oil is thick enough to block oilways and clog filters, and will certainly not protect your engine as well as good oil.

Supporting the bike

Supporting the bike can be a real headache, especially if it is only equipped with a side stand. This clearly represents a challenge when removing a wheel for a tyre change. If you have a centre stand then life is a little easier, unless your bike is off-balance – heavier on one wheel than the other when on the stand. Whichever method you use, loosen all the necessary fasteners when the bike is still on both wheels, because if you start trying to undo a tight axle nut when the bike is balanced precariously it will fall over!

A bike with only a side stand can be persuaded to support itself with the help of a sturdy stick, or perhaps even some luggage under the bash-plate. If the side stand is in the right place on the bike you can make it work like the leg of a tripod, using the bike's own weight to stabilise it. With the side stand deployed, use a luggage strap to tie the handlebars on full lock. If you have hard luggage, remove the pannier from the opposite side to the stand, and place it underneath the other pannier. Push the bike against the stand and it will start to lift the front wheel off the ground. Keep pushing until you reach the critical balance point, then carefully lower the bike until the remaining fixed pannier rests on the other one. The bike is now supported on the side stand, the rear wheel and the pannier, leaving the front wheel well off the ground.

If you have no chance of finding anything to prop the bike up with, as a last resort you can lay the bike over on to its side. This does, however, create its own problems, such as potential fuel and oil leakage, and difficulties in refitting wheel spacers or aligning the brake discs with the caliper without the brake pads falling out.

← Supporting a bike on a tree stump...
📷 Author

← ...or on a wooden stake.
📷 Touratech

Picking up a bike

📷 Steve Mills

1 With luggage removed, grasp the lowest bar-end.

2 Keep your back straight and lift the bike...

3 ...using the strength of your thigh muscles.

If you are dealing with the rear wheel, move the chain tension adjustment blocks out of the way so you can move the wheel as far forward as possible in the swing arm. With the tension relieved from the chain you can then lift it off the sprocket and put it to one side, out of the way. The rear wheel, in particular, is fairly heavy and can be a little awkward to manoeuvre, so supporting from above while withdrawing the axle will prevent it tipping and jamming. The inside faces of the swing arm will keep any spacers in place when the axle is finally removed, but be aware that they may fall out of the hub when the wheel is released. Note the order in which they came out, as well as the orientation of any other spacers and seals or covers as reinstalling them in the wrong place can cause misalignment of the wheel. With the wheel released, you should be able to simply lower it and roll it backwards out of the swing arm. Remove the sprocket carrier and any cush-drive rubbers inside the hub and put them safely to one side.

Refitting is the opposite of removal, but take care to get the spacers and bearing covers in the right order in the wheel hub. If it is difficult relocating the wheel, check that the sprocket carrier is correctly seated in the hub. Feed the wheel axle through the swing arm and into the wheel hub, and loosely fasten the axle nut on the other side. Make sure the axle is as far forward in the swing-arm slot as possible as this will allow you to reinstall the chain, then pull the wheel fully back and seat the chain tension adjuster blocks. Push the wheel forward against the chain tension adjuster blocks to ensure that the previous adjustment is maintained, then tighten the axle nut until it is just snug to hold the wheel while you check the wheel alignment, and adjust if necessary. Once everything is straight and checked, tighten the axle nut to the specified torque.

Removing the front wheel is a similar process, taking equal care with the ABS ring and sensor. Removal of the brake calipers will make extracting the wheel much easier and involves only two bolts, but care must be taken to prevent inadvertent operation of the brake lever as this will pump out the slave-cylinder pistons. With the axle nut removed, withdraw the axle while supporting the wheel and lower it to the ground. Check for wheel spacers or bearing covers and slip them on to the axle for safekeeping.

Refitting is a simple reversal of the process, having replaced any spacers or bearing covers in the wheel hub in the order in which they were removed. Lift the wheel into position, slide the axle through the hub and loosely tighten the axle nut. Refit the brake calipers and torque the fasteners accordingly. Tighten and torque the axle nut, finally spinning the wheel to ensure that it runs without binding. With both front and rear brakes, you must pump the brake lever and/or foot pedal several times to reset the brake pads on to the disc surface.

The integral shaft drive and on-board brakes make removing an R1200GS wheel an absolute breeze – simply undo the five bolts securing the wheel to the hub and remove the rear wheel, leaving the brake disc and caliper in place on the shaft-drive housing.

↑↘ Being able to repair punctures is an essential skill.
📷 Touratech

In general, axle bolts will be tightened with a high degree of torque, so you also need to apply a lot of torque to remove them. Make sure all the critical bolts and fasteners are loosened while the bike is still stable on firm ground – if you apply high leverage to a fastener while the bike is in an unstable position it could roll off the stand, with the added risk of trapping you underneath it as it falls. If an anti-lock braking system (ABS) is fitted, dismount and secure the wheel-rotation sensors. Take great care not to damage either the sensor or the sender ring as they are fragile and easily harmed if knocked.

The way a tyre deflates can sometimes be an indicator of what the problem is likely to be. Rapid deflation is clearly the consequence of a puncture. If, on the other hand, deflation is slow, the valve core might be the problem, so identifying that first will obviously avoid the need to take the tyre off the rim.

Checking the valve is easy: simply inflate the tyre as normal and remove the valve cap. Spit on your finger and rub it over the top of the valve stem – if it bubbles, then you have a leaky or loose valve core that is letting air escape from the tube. Your puncture repair kit should contain a tool to remove the valve core, and a spare core too. Check that the core is tight in the valve stem; even if the valve core is sound it will still leak if loose. If it is loose, retighten and reinflate, then recheck with the spit test. If it is tight, then remove it and give it a blow to dislodge anything that might be holding it open – a drop of WD40 is good here too – then replace the valve core and reinflate the tyre. If the valve still leaks, install the new valve core and throw the old one away. If it does not work now, it will not work next time, so there is no point keeping it. Reinflate the tyre and do the spit test; all should be well. If the tyre deflates with a good valve then you definitely have a puncture and will need to repair it.

Tubeless tyres

Any roadside repair to a tubeless tyre must be considered temporary, and the tyre should be properly repaired at the earliest possible opportunity. Repairing a puncture in a tubeless tyre is relatively simple when compared to a tube

repair, however, as in the majority of cases the repair can be effected with the tyre still on the rim, and very often with the wheel still on the bike too.

Various types of tubeless repair kits are available. The simplest uses pre-glued rubber cords commonly called 'gummy worms', while others use a more sophisticated rubber profile, but both utilise the same basic principle of plugging the hole. Using these kits is fairly straightforward once the spike has been removed. Using the tool supplied with the kit, roughen the area to be repaired by inserting the tool into the puncture. Attach the plug or worm to the tool and, if required, generously apply any additional adhesive. Push the plug into the hole with the insertion tool, then withdraw the tool. The plug should stay in the hole, forming the repair. After 30 minutes or so the repair should have cured sufficiently, so simply cut off the protruding part of the plug flush with the surface of the tyre. When the tyre is reinflated, the air pressure will force the plug against the inside surface of the tyre, further strengthening the seal.

If you have to remove a tubeless tyre, one of your biggest challenges will be reseating the bead. Tubeless tyres need a high volume of air flowing into the carcass to press the sidewalls against the wheel rim with sufficient force to create the airtight seal needed to start reinflation. If your tyres have a stiff construction this may not be a problem, but a softer tyre may never have a hard enough contact with the wheel to retain the air that you pump in. There are various methods to achieve this. Some people suggest using a ratchet strap around the circumference of the tyre to squeeze it and push

Tubeless tyre repair

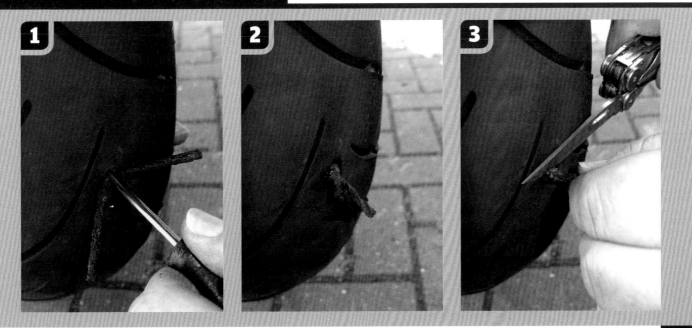

the sidewalls out, while others advocate the use of a partially inflated bicycle tyre inner tube to create a secondary but temporary seal. However, with the risk of being unable to reseat the bead and/or running out of inflation gas canisters, the easiest and perhaps most dependable solution would be to use an inner tube in the conventional way.

Removing tyres

This will probably be one of the most challenging operations you face on the bike, especially if the tyres have not been removed for a while. Invariably they will tend to 'dry' on to the rim, and 'breaking the bead', or getting the tyre to slip off the edge of the rim, can be quite difficult, especially for tubeless tyres. The key here is patience and a little lubrication. Once the wheel is off the bike, make sure that spacers, axle washer and axle nut are kept together, and in the right order, then put them to one side and well out of the way of your operation. Using a tarp sheet will stop any dirt or grit getting into the wheel while you are working on it as well as keeping you off the ground.

Loosen any rim bolts on the wheel, remove the valve cap and valve stem locknut, then deflate the tyre. Remove the valve core too, if you can, as this makes it much easier to empty the tube completely – you might find that the valve cap has a small tool built into it for this purpose. Put these parts carefully in a very safe place. Finally, identify the position of the valve relative to the tyre with a piece of tape; if you have balanced wheels then you can remount the tyre in the same position on the rim.

By now the tyre should be fairly flexible, so start by using your hands or feet to try to push it off the rim – if you are lucky you will get it to slip a little and that will help get you started. Lubrication is also important here, and will make a huge difference to how easily the tyre comes off the rim. Anything is better than nothing – even water – although something slippery is ideal.

Always start at the closest point to the valve, pushing the tyre away from the rim and squirting some lube in between. Move another 15–20cm around the rim and do the same again. Try to work the tyre away from the rim using your tyre levers, remembering that it is much easier if you take small 'bites' rather than one large chunk. Each time you move the tyre, squirt a little more lubricant into the gap – this will creep under the tyre and help lubricate the next section. Once the tyre starts to move off the rim the rest is usually plain sailing.

If you cannot get the tyre off the rim or 'break the bead' manually, you can try a method that is favoured by many people and is quite simple to achieve if a second bike is available. With the second bike vertical, deploy its side stand. Place the wheel with the tyre underneath the stand so that the foot of the stand is as close to the wheel rim as possible. Pull the bike to the side so that the stand now bears down on the tyre's sidewall and that will help press the tyre off the rim. With one section of the tyre's bead broken from the rim the rest will follow quite easily, with just a little help from your boot heel.

With the tyre bead unseated, apply lubricant generously

Tubed tyre repair

to both the tyre and the rim, then start levering the tyre off the rim at the valve while pushing the opposite side of the tyre deep into the well. Taking small sections with the levers requires much less effort, and by the time you reach the 'quarter to two' position the tyre will come off the rim very readily.

If you have tubed tyres, release the valve stem locknut and push the stem into the tyre and recover the tube. If you need the tyre completely off the rim, again use generous amounts of lubricant and pull the rim through the tyre.

Tubed tyres

Using the techniques described in the sections above, remove the wheel so you can take a good look to identify where the puncture is and what caused it. Take a close look at the tyre, checking between the tread blocks. Something like a nail will be fairly obvious and quite visible, but a thorn will be harder to see as it could have broken off, or might even have been pushed right through the tyre. If the offending spike has become dislodged, once the tyre has been removed you will have to partially reinflate the tube in order to see better where the hole is. With enough air in the tube to stretch it and support itself, simply slide your hand around the tyre – you should be able to hear the leaking air hiss as your fingers cover the hole, and you might also be able to feel the stream of air as it will be a lot cooler than the air around you. If the hole is not visibly obvious, you will need to mark the position of the puncture so that you know where to put the patch.

Your puncture repair kit should contain everything needed to repair the tube: sandpaper or an abrasive scraper to prepare the surface of the tube; liquid rubber glue or vulcanising solution; a selection of patches; and possibly a small grey cube of French chalk.

The first thing to do is remove whatever it was that punctured the tyre – and check the inside of the tyre too, to make sure there is nothing sticking through that could not be seen from the outside. With the scraper or sandpaper, roughen the surface of the tube to about 5cm each side of the puncture, making sure the roughened area is at least 2cm larger than the area of the selected repair patch. Apply a reasonable amount of the rubber solution to the roughened area of the inner tube, and rub it in with a fingertip. This will need to dry for a few minutes before applying the patch.

Select a patch that will give at least 2cm coverage around the hole, so use a 4cm patch for a 'regular' puncture and a larger one for a bigger hole or tear. The patch will have two backings: one side will be thick metal foil and the other will be thin plastic film. The metal foil covers the adhesive part of the patch, while the plastic side gives a nice smooth surface to press the patch down with. Note also that the edge of the patch is finely feathered, which helps prevent it lifting once it has been fixed in place.

When the rubber solution has dried to a 'tacky' surface, the patch can be fixed. Remove the foil backing, and hold the patch by the plastic backing. The repair will be strongest if the patch is correctly centred over the hole as this will

give maximum repair strength, so offer the patch to the hole and press it into position. There will be an immediate bond between the patch and the tube. Once it is in place it cannot safely be removed without repeating the whole operation, so try to get it right first time.

With the patch in place, you need to set it properly into position. Stretch the tube gently over your knee, or another hard surface, and use a screwdriver handle or the nose of your tyre lever to press the patch really hard on to the tube. Start from the centre of the patch and work your way outwards to the edge of the patch, ensuring that the feathered edge is firmly stuck down. Leaving the plastic backing in place makes this quite easy. If the edge of the patch lifts a little when you remove the plastic backing, rub it a little more to try to get it to stick, and if necessary apply a little more rubber solution to achieve this. Leave the repair to 'cure' for a few minutes, then pinch the patch to crack the plastic film and remove this from the centre outwards. If your kit contained a cube of chalk, use the sandpaper or abrasive scraper on it and lightly dust the repair area, covering the surplus adhesive so that it will not stick to the inside face of the tyre.

Refitting tyres

Replacement is virtually the reverse of the removal process. Once you have aligned any marks made to help keep the wheel's balance correct, and checked the direction of rotation of the tyre, simply reintroduce the rim into the tyre. For single disc wheels, make sure that you complete the non-disc side of the wheel first – that way the delicate disc will be uppermost (and therefore off the ground and out of danger) when you need to put effort into mounting the tyre. Use a generous amount of lubricant and you will probably find that the first side will slip on to the wheel with very little effort indeed. Turn the wheel over and reinstall the tube, holding the valve stem in place with the locknut. Check and align your marks, then push the tyre bead into the well of the rim opposite the valve. Be generous with the lubricant again, and push the tyre over the rim, working your way evenly each way up each side of the tyre.

Start to use your levers at about the 'quarter to two' position, again tackling a small section each time. Take your time with this task, and make sure that you do not pinch the inner tube between the rim and your tyre lever, otherwise there will be another hole to fix! As long as the bead of the tyre is set right into the well of the wheel rim you should not need too much force, and remember the lubricant – it does make a lot of difference. If everything has gone to plan, the tyre should slip into place just at the valve stem.

Reinflate the tyre to the recommended pressure and check that the bead is correctly seated on the rim by making sure that the moulded line around the tyre wall is parallel to the wheel rim. If there is an area where the bead has not seated completely, try deflating the tyre slightly and bouncing it on the ground and then reinflating. Very often this will help the tyre bead slip into place.

Tubed tyre repair

Wheel bearing failure

7

Even if you replaced your wheel bearings as part of your pre-trip preparations, there is still a chance of suffering bearing failure at some point during your journey.

Repeated water crossings, heavy loads and rough roads will take their toll on even the highest quality wheel bearings and it is prudent to check them regularly. If you are setting out on a long trip it is worth taking a spare set of wheel bearings and the basic tools needed to fit them.

Fortunately replacing wheel bearings is quite a straightforward task and is readily achievable should the need arise.

See pages 102–103 for replacement procedure

← A wheel bearing can fail with little warning.
📷 Greg Baker

Brake pad failure

8

Many miles of off-road riding in dusty or sandy conditions will wear out a set of brake pads in very little time indeed, especially if you are an aggressive rider or your bike is heavily loaded. Like wheel bearings, brake pads are small and compact items that take up little room in your luggage, so having a set ready to install will save the headache of trying to find some, or even the last resort of having some made. Some brake systems are designed so that the pads can be changed without having to remove the calipers, but sometimes the ease of access that comes from unbolting the caliper is more than worth the extra few minutes it takes. Doing this also lets you inspect the condition of the seals and piston, as well as giving you the opportunity of cleaning out any road debris.

See pages 44–87 for bike-specific procedures

← Not many miles left in these pads...
📷 Greg Baker

Chain damage

9

If your chain is in reasonably good condition from the outset, the most likely damage you will experience will be a separated side plate. Broken side plates are rare, unless you are using a low-quality chain, but both eventualities will need a similar repair technique. Use the chain tool to separate the broken link from the rest of the chain and remove both side plates. Rejoin the length of chain using a spring link, remembering the 'O' rings, and ensuring the closed end of the spring clip faces the direction of chain travel. If the damage is more extensive, then two lengths of chain can be joined using a pair of spring links, although replacement should be considered at the earliest possible opportunity.

See pages 90–91 for repair procedure

← A chain with this kind of failure can be repaired for the short term but must be replaced as soon as possible.
📷 Greg Baker

The first indication that you have a cooling problem will probably be the flashing red light on the dash panel indicating that the engine is overheating. The most common causes of overheating will be failure of the cooling system thermostat, or loss of coolant from a hose failure or a radiator breakage This is a critical indicator and the cause *must* be investigated and resolved, otherwise there is a significant risk of serious engine damage. In every case extreme caution must be taken as the coolant will be at a very high temperature and can cause serious burns, and no work should be undertaken until the system is depressurised and safely cool.

Hoses

Cooling system hoses will degrade over time, becoming soft and elastic. As the cooling system is pressurised when it is running at operating temperature, there is a risk of a hose 'ballooning' and developing a hole or a split through which the coolant will leak. This will generally be quite obvious as the escaping liquid will be hissing and steaming. An effective temporary repair can be effected with special radiator hose repair tape which bonds itself to the hose as it gets hot and seals the leak. If the leak or hole is too big to be fixed with tape, you may need to cut the hose at the point of the leak and insert a short length of pipe or even a socket to bridge the gap, then top up the system with water to replace the lost coolant. When secured with hose clips, this fix will last long enough to get you to a workshop to get a proper repair done.

Thermostat

The thermostat is a small device in the cooling system that controls the flow of coolant through the radiator. When the engine is cold it remains closed, preventing coolant reaching the radiator and allowing the engine to rapidly get to operating temperature. As the operating temperature is reached – usually around 90°C – the thermostat will open to allow the coolant to circulate through the radiator. When a thermostat stops working it will usually fail to open, preventing coolant circulating through the radiator, resulting in a serious overheating condition. If this happens, wait until the engine has cooled sufficiently to depressurise the system then simply remove the thermostat from its housing. Top up the coolant with fresh water to replace any lost fluid. The bike will run quite happily without a thermostat, but in cooler conditions it might take longer to reach operating temperature.

Radiator

The most likely problem with the radiator is a puncture or hole caused by a rock or pebble thrown up by the front wheel. There are many tales about using egg white or black pepper in the radiator to seal the leak – these 'repairs' might even work but the reality is that you are unlikely to have the ingredients to hand in the middle of the Sahara! If you have holed a radiator core, the best repair will probably be epoxy putty or chemical metal pushed into the leak to seal it.

➔ **Radiator damage is not often obvious until it is too late. Fitting a radiator guard will help to protect against this kind of impact damage.**

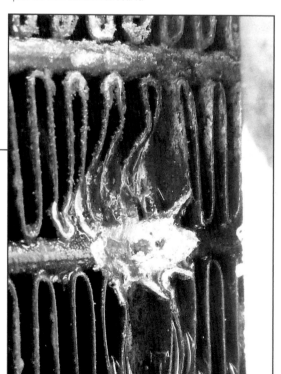

Conversion factors

Length (distance)

Inches (in)	x 25.4	= Millimetres (mm)	x 0.0394	= Inches (in)
Feet (ft)	x 0.305	= Metres (m)	x 3.281	= Feet (ft)
Miles	x 1.609	= Kilometres (km)	x 0.621	= Miles

Volume (capacity)

Cubic inches (cu in; in^3)	x 16.387	= Cubic centimetres (cc; cm^3)	x 0.061	= Cubic inches (cu in; in^3)
Imperial pints (Imp pt)	x 0.568	= Litres (l)	x 1.76	= Imperial pints (Imp pt)
Imperial quarts (Imp qt)	x 1.137	= Litres (l)	x 0.88	= Imperial quarts (Imp qt)
Imperial quarts (Imp qt)	x 1.201	= US quarts (US qt)	x 0.833	= Imperial quarts (Imp qt)
US quarts (US qt)	x 0.946	= Litres (l)	x 1.057	= US quarts (US qt)
Imperial gallons (Imp gal)	x 4.546	= Litres (l)	x 0.22	= Imperial gallons (Imp gal)
Imperial gallons (Imp gal)	x 1.201	= US gallons (US gal)	x 0.833	= Imperial gallons (Imp gal)
US gallons (US gal)	x 3.785	= Litres (l)	x 0.264	= US gallons (US gal)

Mass (weight)

Ounces (oz)	x 28.35	= Grams (g)	x 0.035	= Ounces (oz)
Pounds (lb)	x 0.454	= Kilograms (kg)	x 2.205	= Pounds (lb)

Force

Ounces-force (ozf; oz)	x 0.278	= Newtons (N)	x 3.6	= Ounces-force (ozf; oz)
Pounds-force (lbf; lb)	x 4.448	= Newtons (N)	x 0.225	= Pounds-force (lbf; lb)
Newtons (N)	x 0.1	= Kilograms-force (kgf; kg)	x 9.81	= Newtons (N)

Pressure

Pounds-force per square inch (psi; lbf/in^2; lb/in^2)	x 0.070	= Kilograms-force per square centimetre (kgf/cm^2; kg/cm^2)	x 14.223	= Pounds-force per square inch (psi; lbf/in^2; lb/in^2)
Pounds-force per square inch (psi; lbf/in^2; lb/in^2)	x 0.068	= Atmospheres (atm)	x 14.696	= Pounds-force per square inch (psi; lbf/in^2; lb/in^2)
Pounds-force per square inch (psi; lbf/in^2; lb/in^2)	x 0.069	= Bars	x 14.5	= Pounds-force per square inch (psi; lbf/in^2; lb/in^2)
Pounds-force per square inch (psi; lbf/in^2; lb/in^2)	x 6.895	= Kilopascals (kPa)	x 0.145	= Pounds-force per square inch (psi; lbf/in^2; lb/in^2)
Kilopascals (kPa)	x 0.01	= Kilograms-force per square centimetre (kgf/cm^2; kg/cm^2)	x 98.1	= Kilopascals (kPa)
Millibar (mbar)	x 100	= Pascals (Pa)	x 0.01	= Millibar (mbar)
Millibar (mbar)	x 0.0145	= Pounds-force per square inch (psi; lbf/in^2; lb/in^2)	x 68.947	= Millibar (mbar)
Millibar (mbar)	x 0.75	= Millimetres of mercury (mmHg)	x 1.333	= Millibar (mbar)
Millibar (mbar)	x 0.401	= Inches of water (inH$_2$O)	x 2.491	= Millibar (mbar)
Millimetres of mercury (mmHg)	x 0.535	= Inches of water (inH$_2$O)	x 1.868	= Millimetres of mercury (mmHg)
Inches of water (inH$_2$O)	x 0.036	= Pounds-force per square inch (psi; lbf/in^2; lb/in^2)	x 27.68	= Inches of water (inH$_2$O)

Torque (moment of force)

Pounds-force inches (lbf in; lb in)	x 1.152	= Kilograms-force centimetre (kgf cm; kg cm)	x 0.868	= Pounds-force inches (lbf in; lb in)
Pounds-force inches (lbf in; lb in)	x 0.113	= Newton metres (Nm)	x 8.85	= Pounds-force inches (lbf in; lb in)
Pounds-force inches (lbf in; lb in)	x 0.083	= Pounds-force feet (lbf ft; lb ft)	x 12	= Pounds-force inches (lbf in; lb in)
Pounds-force feet (lbf ft; lb ft)	x 0.138	= Kilograms-force metres (kgf m; kg m)	x 7.233	= Pounds-force feet (lbf ft; lb ft)
Pounds-force feet (lbf ft; lb ft)	x 1.356	= Newton metres (Nm)	x 0.738	= Pounds-force feet (lbf ft; lb ft)
Newton metres (Nm)	x 0.102	= Kilograms-force metres (kgf m; kg m)	x 9.804	= Newton metres (Nm)

Power

Horsepower (hp)	x 745.7	= Watts (W)	x 0.0013	= Horsepower (hp)

Velocity (speed)

Miles per hour (miles/hr; mph)	x 1.609	= Kilometres per hour (km/hr; kph)	x 0.621	= Miles per hour (miles/hr; mph)

Fuel consumption

Miles per gallon, Imperial (mpg)	x 0.354	= Kilometres per litre (km/l)	x 2.825	= Miles per gallon, Imperial (mpg)
Miles per gallon, US (mpg)	x 0.425	= Kilometres per litre (km/l)	x 2.352	= Miles per gallon, US (mpg)

Temperature

Degrees Fahrenheit = (°C x 1.8) + 32   Degrees Celsius (Degrees Centigrade; °C) = (°F - 32) x 0.56